Pirate Arrrt!

Watkins College
of Art & Design

Pirate Arrrt!

Learn to Draw Fantastic Pirates,
Treasure Chests, Ships,
Sea Monsters and More

Rob Mcleay

Ulysses
Press

Copyright © 2008 Rob Mcleay. Copyright design and concept © 2008 Ulysses Press. No part of this publication may be reproduced, stored in a retrieval system, or transmitted in any form or by any means without the prior written permission of the publisher, nor be otherwise circulated in any form of binding or cover other than that in which it is published and without a similar condition being imposed on the subsequent purchaser.

Published by:
ULYSSES PRESS
P.O. Box 3440
Berkeley, CA 94703
www.ulyssespress.com

ISBN10: 1-56975-663-5
ISBN13: 978-1-56975-663-8
Library of Congress Control Number 2007907740

Printed in Canada by Webcom

10 9 8 7 6 5 4 3 2 1

Acquisitions Editor: Nick Denton-Brown
Managing Editor: Claire Chun
Editorial: Lauren Harrison, Scott McRae, Elyce Petker, Emma Silvers
Production: Tamara Kowalski
Cover design: John M. Duggan

Distributed by Publishers Group West

Chapters

Acknowledgments

First, thanks to my lovely wife, Seeger, for supporting me through my first book (hopefully one of many!) and to my pirate dog, Jose the Schnauzer. I would like to thank my man at Ulysses Press, Captain Nick Blackbeard, and Cabin Girl Lauren for pushing me to my limits and not expecting anything less than superb.

Introduction

I have been drawing for 14 years, doing all sorts of work—from storyboarding on movies to general illustration work to teaching. I have found that even though I have been drawing since I was 18, I am always learning new techniques and passing them on to my students. The best bit of advice I can give is to draw because it makes you feel good and draw from the heart.

To all the budding artists that have invested in my book, I hope you enjoy reading it as much as I have enjoyed creating it! While writing this book, sometimes I would wake up in the middle of the night speaking in pirate tongue and start looking for my gold.

Please visit my website, www.thedrawingstudio.co.nz for pirate DVDs and online tutorials. You can also download movies onto your computer to watch whenever you'd like.

Shiver me timbers…arrrrr,

Captain Rob "Purple Beard" Mcleay
New Zealand
August 2008

Chapter 1
Drawing Pirate Details

Drawing Two-Point Perspective

Step One

Begin by drawing a horizontal line with a mark on both ends.

Horizontal line

Step Two

Draw a vertical line (B) as shown below and then draw lines (A) and (C). From Point 1, very lightly draw a guide line to the top of (A), (B) and (C). Do the same with Point 2. Now draw in some random lines that will help create parts of the house later on.

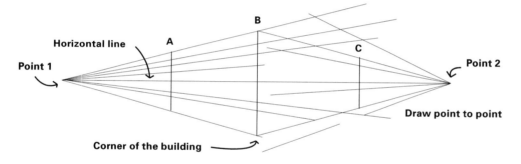

Horizontal line

Point 1

A

B

C

Point 2

Draw point to point

Corner of the building

Step Three

You can begin to add the smaller details such as the roof and windows. Take note of how both windows have guide lines that AIM toward the two points we drew earlier. The chimney has been dragged out to show that if you draw correctly in 3D, you can snap objects in or out.

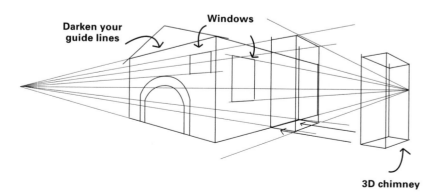

Darken your guide lines

Windows

3D chimney

Final rendering

Two-point sketch

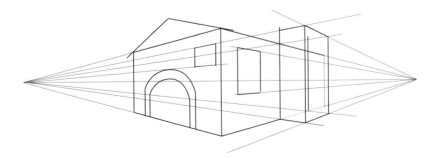

Generating Ideas for Character Design

So you are sitting there with a blank piece of paper, 23 different types of pencils, possibly a ruler and sawdust representing your imagination. There is a way of kick-starting the process of generating ideas, and all it comes down to is picking up that pencil and starting to scribble. Do this for about 15 minutes, and before you know it you will have a couple pages of unique designs that you can incorporate into your characters.

Generating ideas for character design can be started in the same way. I tend to draw quick 30-second poses that have very minimal detail but have a lot of shapes. I will draw this way until my designs look strong and well balanced. It also helps to know the personality of the character which, believe it or not, can be drawn into the design! Other things to think about are the height and weight of the characters and what sort of action you want them to be in: are they walking, running, lying down, etc. Check out the rough doodling I did to generate ideas for this book.

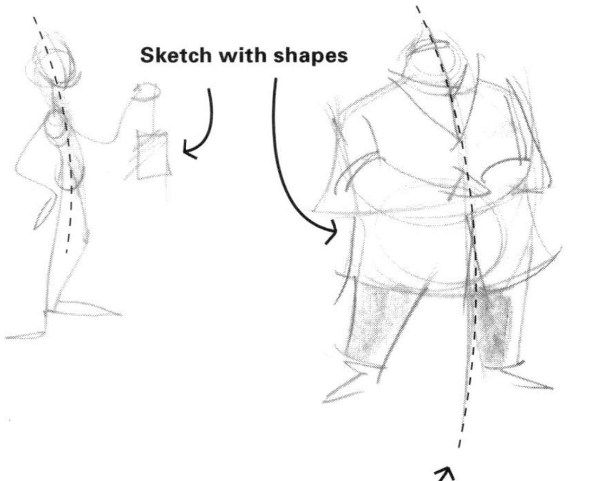

Sketch with shapes

Line of action

Keep doodles to 30 seconds

The more sketches the better

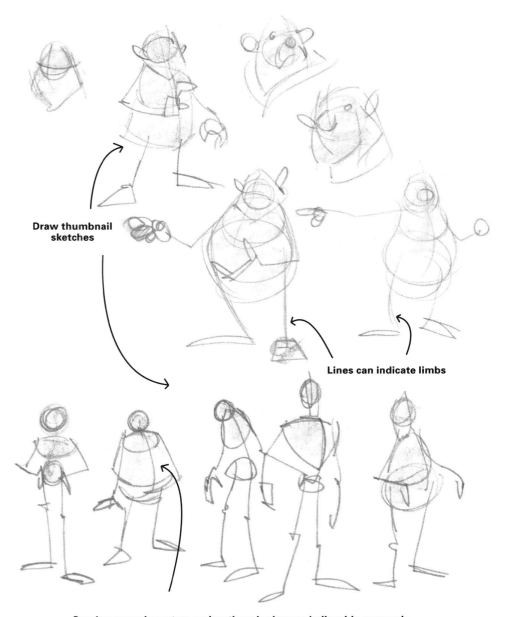

Draw thumbnail sketches

Lines can indicate limbs

Curving your characters makes them look more believable as people. Have you ever seen a person with no arch in their back? The same rule applies to your human cartoons

I will draw like this until I have achieved two things. The first is that I have loosened up enough to draw my characters better. If you try and draw a masterpiece right off the bat without a warm-up, you will end up drawing something that looks stiff. With half an hour of warm-up, your drawings will look relaxed and natural! The second goal I want to achieve is having a small library of poses to pick and choose from. Also, if you are creating some artwork for someone, you can show them the poses and ask them what they like the most. This will save you a lot of time and grief in the future.

Interpreting the Tutorial Breakdowns

This section explains how to interpret my drawing tutorials. I have used various techniques in order to show you how to construct your drawings from scratch to the final rendering. Some of these techniques, though, are only there to aid you in getting to the end. Some of the line work that you will see in these tutorials is a lot darker than you would normally draw.

When you began your career as an artist, you probably got your inspiration off the old cartoons on TV and then tried to recreate the amazing artwork on the closest scrap of paper with a half-chewed coloring pencil. I bet that you tried to get the character looking absolutely perfect the first time around, with no mistakes, no extra lines, no nothing except a nice piece of slick artwork. There is nothing wrong with this as art, since drawing is a subjective topic and artists can always draw how they want. But in order to progress and speed up your drawings and take them to that next level, you need to attack them in a different way. That's what I will be showing you in Pirate Arrt!

The first thing I think about when drawing a cartoon character, or a even a background landscape scene, are the shapes that I will be using to create my masterpiece. Look at the example I have drawn. You will see that I have begun with a few shapes. This is where I need you to concentrate, because I can only write this once (I have a space mission to launch shortly). Look at the line work of the shapes and see how dark and crisp I have drawn them. Do NOT draw your construction lines like this! I have used a graphic software program to create this technique for purely cosmetic reasons. What I want you to do is to look at the drawing next to it and draw your lines like that. Remember to draw LIGHTLY when beginning your drawing, because you will NOT be using all the lines you just created. Only darken your lines when you are absolutely happy with where they are. The reason I have used this method throughout the book is simply to help you visualize what I see in my head when I am drawing. I do not draw dark lines from the beginning. If you still don't quite get it, look at the example below and you will see what I mean!

Light rough lines

Begin like this

Cosmetic purposes only

But visualize like this

End up like this!

Basic Construction
Turning Shapes Into Objects

Throughout this book you will come across a lot of different shapes in a multitude of forms. Some of them will make sense and some will look completely out of whack. You may think to yourself, "They don't have shapes drawn on the TV characters, so why do I need to draw with shapes here?" First of all, GREAT QUESTION! The reason I use shapes to begin my drawings is to help make the drawings look better. Another one of the reasons is just to make sure that every part of the body is in its correct place before we go and add the detail. It also helps with proportions, as we don't want a character whose head looks like a lollipop on a stick. Below are a few examples of what you will see in the book and how to transition from shapes to detail.

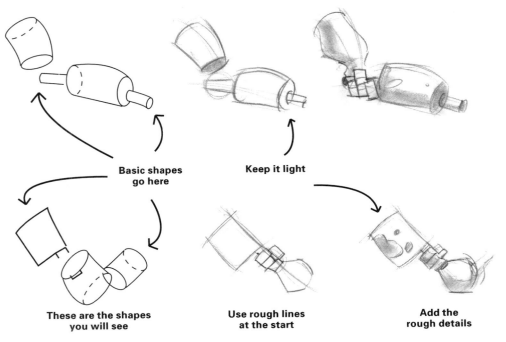

**Basic shapes
go here**

Keep it light

**These are the shapes
you will see**

**Use rough lines
at the start**

**Add the
rough details**

Rendering

Having basic rendering skills (shading) will take your drawing skills to another level. It will transform a flat, two-dimensional drawing into a vivid, alive, three-dimensional piece of great art! Below are three examples of rendering techniques that I use when drawing. The first example is hatched: this is where you draw a heck of a lot of lines on the same angle. The second example is cross-hatched: simply hatching at two different angles. The last example is using the side of the pencil: this is where you get the most coverage and can cover large amounts of surface quickly.

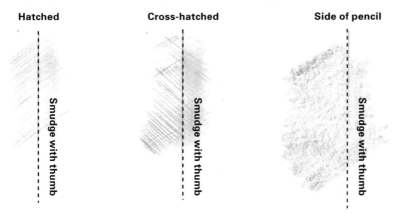

Hatched　　　　**Cross-hatched**　　　　**Side of pencil**

Smudge with thumb

You will notice a dashed line through the middle of the shading. The pencil work on the is a technique I call smudging, which you do with your fat thumb! Smudging can give a nice airbrushed effect, which helps give the drawing a professional look.

The next set of examples are rendered balls. Instead of drawing a flat 2D circle, add some shadow to the circle to give the impression of form.

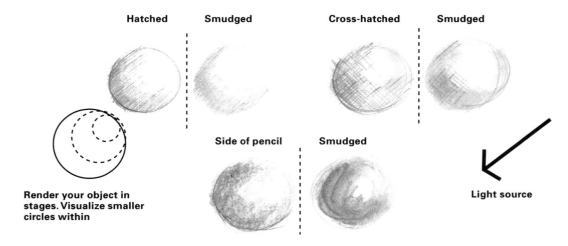

Hatched　　**Smudged**　　　　**Cross-hatched**　　**Smudged**

Render your object in stages. Visualize smaller circles within

Side of pencil　　**Smudged**

Light source

Identifying the Light Source

When you begin to render your object or subject, you need to identify which direction the light source is coming from. The light source can be anything that emits light, such as the sun, light bulbs or even reflections from other objects nearby.

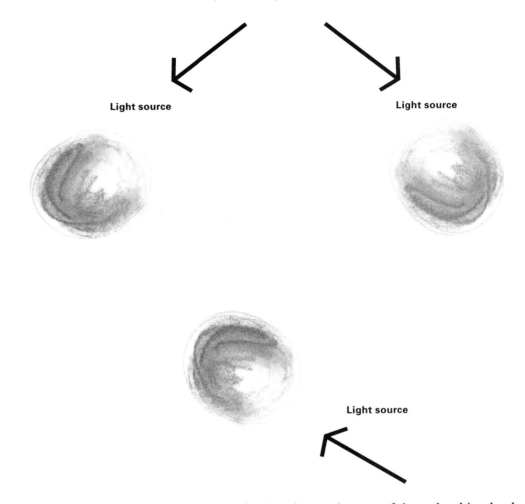

The next step to creating a fantastic piece of art is to know what sort of shape the object has been drawn with. Is it a tube or is it a sphere? This will determine how you need to shade your picture. In the above example it is a sphere, so the shadow will WRAP around the circle.

Coloring Your Drawings

You will find that, after doing a lot of pencil drawings, you tend to forget to add color to what you are doing. If you don't get yourself into color and start to practice this skill, your drawings may lack that "X" factor later on. Maybe that big animation company you just scored a job with will get you to draw the grass on background #4537, instead of hiring you as the lead character designer who sits upstairs in a comfy seat with the director, sipping Kool-Aid.

Begin your coloring career by sticking with some fundamental basics. Copy NATURE. Mother Nature knows how to color—just stick your big head out the window for a second and look at the nearest tree. Look at the way the sun reflects off the leaves, and check out the shadows they cast onto others—get the idea? Using color takes a while to master and you will have a lot more so-so drawings than top-notch ones in the beginning, but don't despair. The more you do it, the more you can avoid mistakes in the future.

Now, there are various ways of adding color to your drawings. The most obvious is using colored pencils, but I also recommend getting into computer software. I use Photoshop and Artrage most of the time, because using software to color can make you draw quicker!

Using Pencils

Let's face it, if there are no pencils in the house, how are you going to draw? It's always a good idea to hide a stash of pencils all over the house because you never know when you might want to draw. Stash them under the couch cushions, in the glass next to the toilet, in the backseat of the car, and even tape them to Fido, your pet dog. (He won't like it, but it will come in handy one day.) Do you get the idea? Have you ever been just sitting by yourself dreaming of marshmallows because there is nothing else to do? Well, imagine that you had stashed a few pencils close by with a wad of paper ready to be drawn on. You could now draw the marshmallows you were just dreaming of! There's nothing worse than having to locate your drawing materials when you are having a creative moment, and then having the moment slip into oblivion before you can get organized.

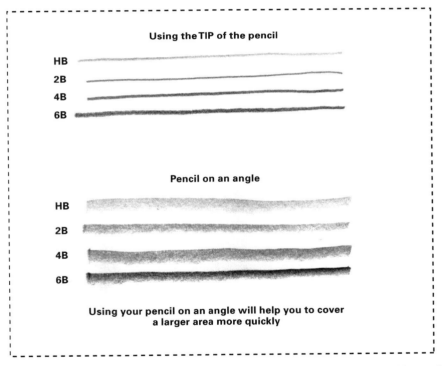

Using the TIP of the pencil

HB

2B

4B

6B

Pencil on an angle

HB

2B

4B

6B

Using your pencil on an angle will help you to cover a larger area more quickly

The pencils I use the most are the HB, the 2B and the 4B. Each pencil has a different softness associated with it. The higher the number on the pencil, the softer it is, and the more mess you make! You can also get pencils that are different widths. These can produce different results depending on how you HOLD the pencil.

Drawing Using Perspective

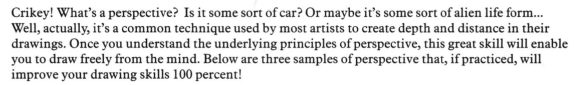

Crikey! What's a perspective? Is it some sort of car? Or maybe it's some sort of alien life form... Well, actually, it's a common technique used by most artists to create depth and distance in their drawings. Once you understand the underlying principles of perspective, this great skill will enable you to draw freely from the mind. Below are three samples of perspective that, if practiced, will improve your drawing skills 100 percent!

Two Point-Perspective

Two point perspective gives the impression of depth, so when you are looking down both sides of this building, it looks as if it's getting farther away.

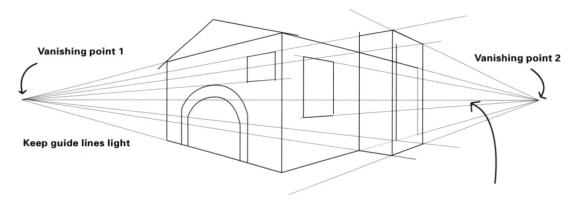

Vanishing point 1

Vanishing point 2

Keep guide lines light

One-Point Perspective

One-point perspective is where you use only one vanishing point for your guide lines to connect to.

Horizon lines

Vanishing point 1

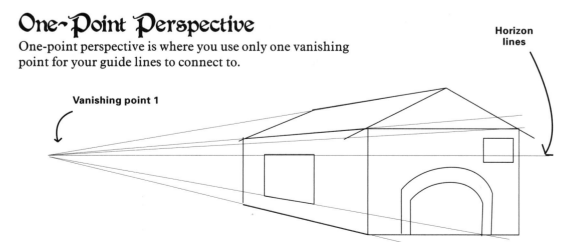

Using Shapes to Create Poses

When I begin a character, I tend to muck around with various shapes and forms. If it is a large man, I lean toward big box shapes. For a thin man, I would use the opposite—a longer, thinner shape. Get it? Take a look at the shapes below and give it a shot.

Tip: If you can draw nice shapes, you can draw great cartoons!

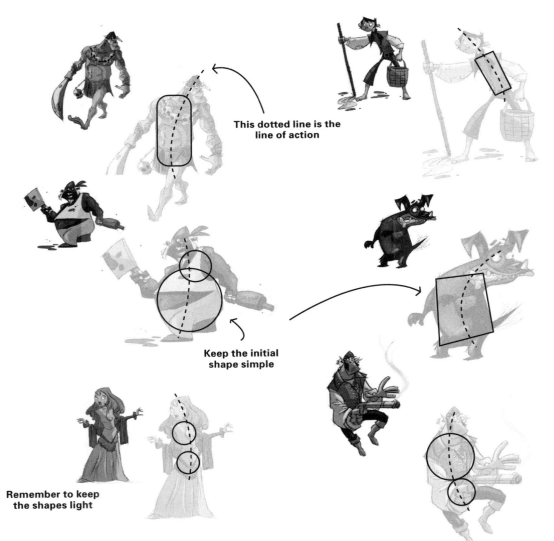

This dotted line is the line of action

Keep the initial shape simple

Remember to keep the shapes light

Why draw a line of action? The line of action is an imaginary line extending through the main action. Once you have the line, you can base your character's entire pose around it. Not having the line of action may make your characters look weak and limp.

Chapter 2
Drawing the Pirates

Drawing the Pirate

In this section, we will be breaking down some really, really hairy pirates, who possibly stink as well, since they tend not to bathe on a regular basis. I will be using the character below to create new facial expressions, showing the ease with which this can be done.

Polka dot bandana? Maybe...

Missing teeth

Pirates love earrings, so pierce away

Give him a moustache and goatee

Stubble looks good

Ripped shirt 'cause he said so

Hairy arms are good

Every pirate needs a sword or sharp object

Drawing the Facial Expressions

Okay, this part takes some time and practice before you will get it right. What I have created is a basic model sheet of facial expressions. This will help you later on when you want your character to change moods, or you want to give him life. Notice how much influence the eyes have on the overall expressions.

"You did what with that?"
This is a surprised look, with wide eyes, raised eyebrows and an open mouth.

"I think I had waaay too many baked beans..."
This is an embarrassed look. The eyes are sheepish and he's checking over his shoulder to see if anyone is looking before he farts.

"Is that what I thought I saw?"
This is a suspicious look. The eyes are squinting and the eyebrows are angry.

"I just pillaged a town."
This is a gleeful look. The eyes are wide, the eyebrows are up, and the mouth is open and ready to yell.

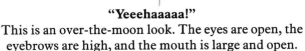

"Yeeehaaaaa!"
This is an over-the-moon look. The eyes are open, the eyebrows are high, and the mouth is large and open.

Using Shapes to Create Random Heads

A great way to get the creative juices flowing is to draw random shapes that can be converted into heads. I often will do this to help me get started. Take a minute to practice with the shapes provided.

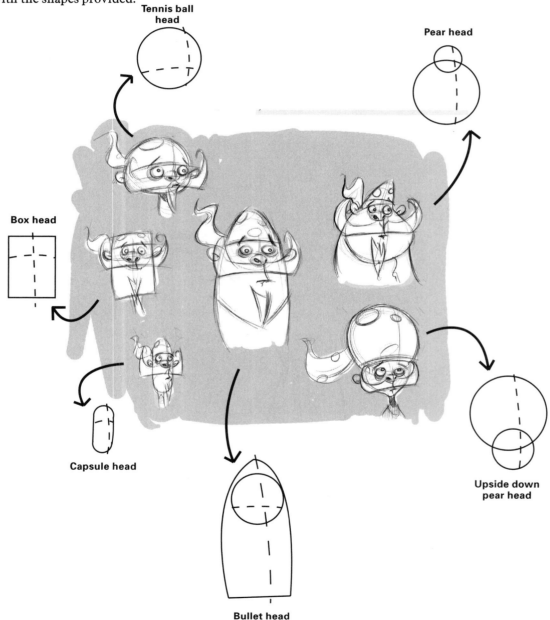

Tennis ball head

Pear head

Box head

Capsule head

Bullet head

Upside down pear head

Drawing Your Character at Different Angles

There is usually a time in your drawing career when you must rotate your character so he (or she) is looking in a different direction. Let's face it, you can only draw Billy Bob the Pirate looking at you in so many drawings—and he's most likely sick of looking at your ugly mug anyway! The key to this skill is to ROTATE the shapes that you have used to create your character. As you can see below, I am using circles to do this.

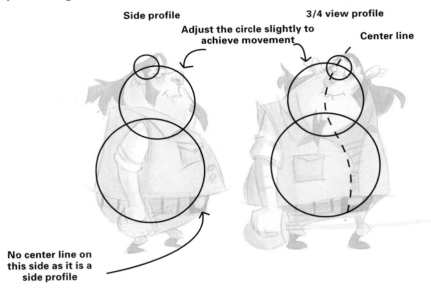

Side profile

3/4 view profile

Adjust the circle slightly to achieve movement

Center line

No center line on this side as it is a side profile

Why do you need a center line? A center line indicates where the center of the character's body is. If the character rotates, the line will rotate too. If you don't have a center line, when turning your character, it will be harder to place the detail that needs to be drawn, such as the buttons on the shirt and the nose on the face.

If you look at me too long, I start to get better looking...

Chapter 3
The Pirate Crew

Angus McAngus
Henchman

Angus likes his sword, so make sure that you take care when drawing it. He also has found himself a couple of pistols that don't really work too well, so they are mainly there for cosmetic reasons.

Step One
The Face

Begin with a rough circle/sphere for his face. Then add in the guide lines for the eyes, nose and mouth. The guide lines will help you to place the face parts correctly so you don't have to keep rubbing out your mistakes.

Always add the guide lines!

Eye line   **The mouth goes 'ere**

Step Two
The Hat

Angus loves to wear his hat whenever he pillages and even when he sleeps, be it a daytime nap or nighttime snooze. Make sure when you draw the hat to overlay it across the circle that we drew for the head. Sketch in the eyeballs and use the same guide line to line the ears up with.

An easy simple shape!

Draw lightly   **Start the hat with this shape**

Then add the curve at the top of the hat

Across the head

Step Three
The Torso

It's usually a good idea to start with a center line going right through Angus's spindly frame. You can call this the LINE OF ACTION or the flow of the character. Sketch in a 3D box for the chest, leave a gap, then add in the pelvis box. I have drawn them in 3D, but if you are struggling with the shape, just draw a FLAT box for now. Draw the hair coming out of the hat.

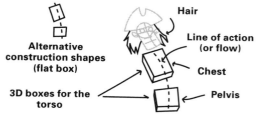

Alternative construction shapes (flat box)

3D boxes for the torso

Hair

Line of action (or flow)

Chest

Pelvis

Step Four
The Limbs of Angus McAngus

Let's draw some ants! You can approach this two ways: hands and feet first or limbs first. I tend to mix it up depending on the complexity of the pose itself. Notice how the right hand is halfway between the foot and the head and also in line with the top of his pelvic shape. The left hand will be slightly higher but generally on the same horizontal line. Also take note of the right hand sitting just past the right foot.

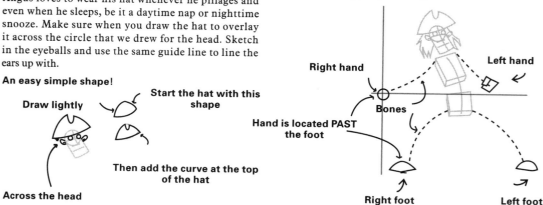

Right hand   **Left hand**

Bones

Hand is located PAST the foot

Right foot   **Left foot**

Step Five
More Limbs of Angus McAngus + Sword!

For this step, let's concentrate on the two arms and him holding the sword. For the right arm I have used one tube, as I didn't see the point in doing two, but the left arm as been broken down into two because of the bend. The fingers look a bit like spider legs on the right hand, but for the left hand start with a block then break it into smaller parts. The sword begins with a tube for the handle and an eclipse-like shape for the blade. (See following page for a breakdown of the sword and how to draw Angus holding it.)

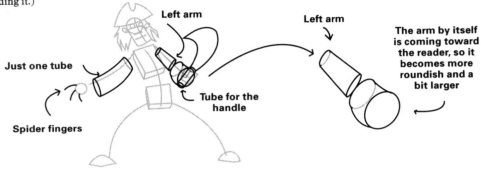

Left arm

Left arm

The arm by itself is coming toward the reader, so it becomes more roundish and a bit larger

Just one tube

Tube for the handle

Spider fingers

Step Six
Legs and Pistols

Overlay tubes for his legs across the bones we drew earlier. These will be quite slim and you may be able to get away with drawing flat shapes if it gets too tricky. The pistols are constructed with tubes and sit nicely over the pelvic area, tucked into his pants.

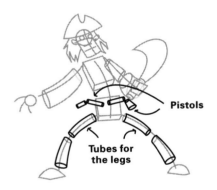

Pistols

Tubes for the legs

Angus McAngus Breakdown

Here are a couple of breakdown sketches that you can practice, with the main thing to remember being to keep it light and draw as much as you can with 3D shapes.

Angus McAngus ~ Extras

Follow these steps to finish the right hand. The main thing to remember here is, when drawing the fingers, think of tubes. This will give the hands a nice 3D feel.

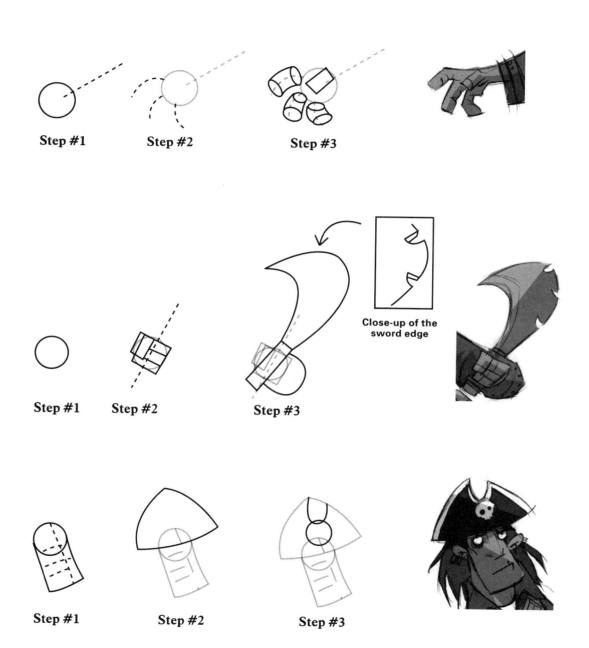

Step #1   **Step #2**   **Step #3**

Close-up of the sword edge

Step #1   **Step #2**   **Step #3**

Step #1   **Step #2**   **Step #3**

Chef Ricky Rooney
Dinner anyone?

Dinner parties are not Chef Ricky Rooney's favorite pastime, but as any good pirate chef would do, he sucks it up and gets the job done. Don't get on his bad side either, as the local rat population will mysteriously decrease and bowel movements will increase.

Breakdown of Chef Ricky Rooney

Ricky is made up of mainly two large spheres (a fancy word for a 3D circle). His body is slightly twisted so it gives a sense of movement. He has been designed in such a way that nothing is symmetrical; i.e., the left arm is doing something different from the right arm. Try and keep this in mind when drawing Ricky, and also try and apply it to your characters in the future.

Step One
The Face

Okay, this character has quite a lot happening so we need to start off with a sphere/circle first, then add in the guide lines (see the first chapter for a reminder on how important it is to draw them in first). Now, starting from the EYE guide line, draw in the shape of the jaw. It's quite similar to a square.

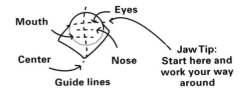

Step Two
Face Detail

When adding the face detail keep in mind that you may need to change it later, so begin light. Start off by drawing in two circles for the eyes, and make sure they are sitting nicely on those guide lines.

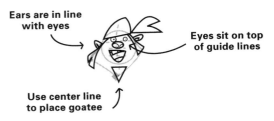

The Nose Walkthrough

Follow this guide on drawing his nose. Start with a rough oval, add the center line and then add an additional two ovals, one on each side of the center line. When you are happy, go ahead and darken the lines.

Step #1   Step #2   Step #3

Use ovals for nostrils

The Mouth Walkthrough

The mouth is constructed with a half oval and its guide line. Roughly add the teeth and tongue lines in, and when you think they look okay, go ahead and commit with some darker lines. I made one tooth bigger to break up the monotony of the teeth.

Step #1   Step #2   Step #3

Step Three
The Torso

Now, chef Ricky Rooney ain't been slimmin' down on the celery and carrots for the last 10 years. His diet consists mostly of pig, beef and chicken, and very rarely will he venture to anything that looks and smells green! How do we draw this oversized man? Simple! Start with a sphere/circle the size of his head for his chest and the same shape but twice as big for his beast of a belly. Notice how I have moved the belly to the left. Bring the center line to the edge of the circle as well, to imply that he is facing left.

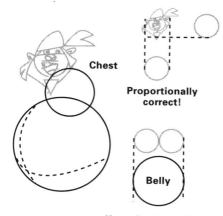

Chest

Proportionally correct!

Belly

Keep the chest the same size as the head

Step Four
Arms and Hands

There is a little trick that I use when I draw arms. Identify where the shoulders sit (see my breakdown) and sketch in a circle for each shoulder. This will help you to start the arms. Now draw the arms.

Meat Cleaver

Begin with a rough rectangle for the blade and a long rectangle for the handle.

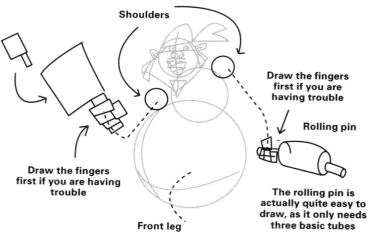

Shoulders

Draw the fingers first if you are having trouble

Rolling pin

Draw the fingers first if you are having trouble

The rolling pin is actually quite easy to draw, as it only needs three basic tubes

Front leg

Every now and then you will come across a character that is holding some sort of object such as a sword, knife, gun, ferret or moose. If you are having trouble with a hand that is holding objects, draw the object first, then WRAP the fingers around it.

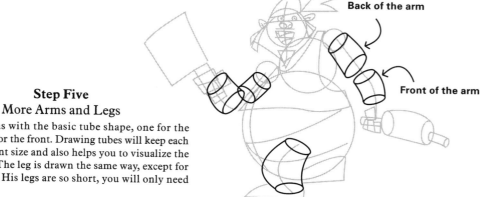

Back of the arm

Front of the arm

Step Five
More Arms and Legs

Begin the arms with the basic tube shape, one for the back and one for the front. Drawing tubes will keep each arm a consistent size and also helps you to visualize the angles easier. The leg is drawn the same way, except for this character. His legs are so short, you will only need one tube.

Captain Blackbeard Turn Around Head

A turn around model sheet is a character in many different poses and angles. Below is a rough turn around design of Blackbeard himself, and further down are the shapes that I used to create him. You will notice that all the shapes are the same, but are just on different angles.

Blackbeard's Beard

This is a PRIME example on why drawing center lines helps you to draw better! When you draw the beard, aim for the center line that you originally drew and duplicate this technique for when you rotate his head.

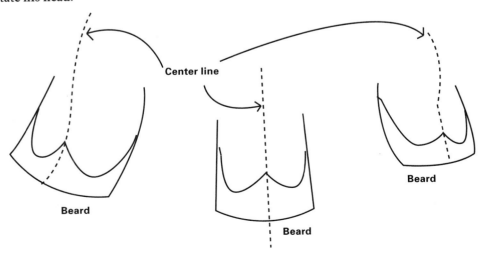

Center line

Beard

Beard

Beard

Damsel in Distress!

Taken from a nearby Navy boat, this damsel is now a prisoner of the mighty Blackbeard! Oh, the thought of peeling potatoes for the next three months at sea may be a bit too much for this beauty!

The Breakdown

After drawing male hair for a while, drawing the opposite sex can get tricky, especially with all those curls. It's even worse when it's windy! A good tip is to practice real-life hairstyles from photographs.

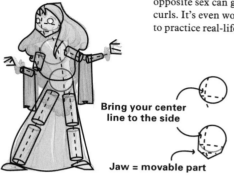

Bring your center line to the side

Jaw = movable part

Step One
The Face

I have broken the damsel's face into two parts for step one. As with all faces, I start with a circle and add a center guide line, so take note that she is looking left and place the guide line on the left side. Add the jaw next. I see it as a moveable part so it's drawn separately. Now add the mouth guide.

Step Two
Female Torso

We can use two circles to start the torso. She has a slight curve in her body, so make sure that you have adjusted the torso shapes to reflect her bend. Since she is facing to the right, the center guide line will be drawn on the right-hand side.

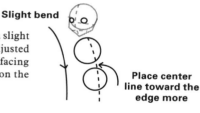

Slight bend

Place center line toward the edge more

Think spider legs

The leg construction and placement help balance the torso and rest of body

Step Three
Arms, Legs 'n' Hands

It's important to plan where your arms and legs are going to end up. If you don't plan this part well, your character may look like she's going to fall over. Notice how balanced she seems. Look at the angle the torso is on and then see how I have balanced her with strategic placements of the legs. The hands are quite tiny, so start off like you are drawing spider legs.

Start here, will ye

Tubes for the arms!

Keep drawing the hair even though it's hidden

Step Four
More Arms and Hair

When you think you are happy with the location and size of the head, begin to draw the hair. For this drawing I am utilizing the circle I created earlier for my starting points. Sometimes you may need to start a fraction higher to give the impression of THICKNESS of the hair. You will notice that where the hair hangs down near the bottom, it curls back up. I've drawn that in to keep the hair looking consistent. The arms can now be drawn in with tubes.

Nothing here but tubes, sir

Step Five
Legs

The legs are quite straightforward here, just plain old tubes to be laid over the guide lines. See how important it is to draw the construction lines in first? You may have to redraw the picture if you didn't use this technique! Now you may be saying to yourself, "Why do I need to draw the legs when I don't see them on the character???" Well, sir or ma'am, the reason is that if your character does not have legs, she will quite simply fall over. Also, it helps with the placement of her dress.

Step Six
The Fabric

Fabric can be quite tricky to draw, because you have to consider many factors, such as the length, weight, texture and the object or person that it is draping over. Notice on the bottom of the Damsel's dress how it wraps itself over the left foot, sags a bit when hitting the ground, and then lifts to go over the right foot. Practice it a few times before drawing it on the character. Now let's concentrate on the scarf and how it hangs straight down. What's happening here is GRAVITY. When there is no wind, there is only one way fabric should hang ...down. Throw in a couple of folds at the end, for a touch of realism.

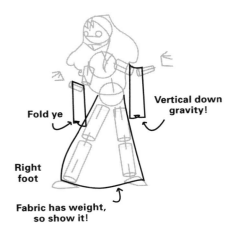

Fold ye

Vertical down gravity!

Right foot

Fabric has weight, so show it!

Damsel Roughs

Here are sketches I did of the Damsel in Distress. The first drawing is of the initial shapes and getting everything in the right area. With the second drawing, I start committing to the line work, sketching a little bit darker.

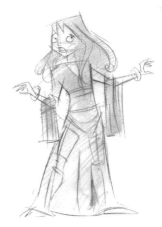

Drawing the Scarf

Step One
Make sure you have drawn in the major torso shape first.

Torso

Step Two
Draw in the guide lines for the scarf.

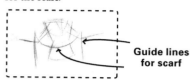

Guide lines for scarf

Step Three
Over the guide lines you will need to add the final detail.

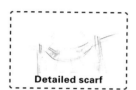

Detailed scarf

Close-up of the details

Scarf hangs straight down

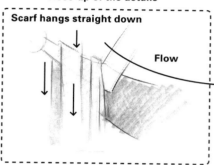

Flow

Sketching in the Details

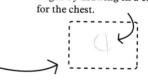

Step One
Begin by drawing in a circle for the chest.

Step Two
Add in the thickness of the chest as shown with the squarish shape below. Add the center line, as this will come in handy later on.

Squarish?... kind of

Step Three
Very lightly draw in a "V" shape starting from the top of the chest and meeting at the center line.

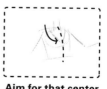

Aim for that center line, will you

Step Four
This is when you can start adding the detail. See the following picture for a more detailed image.

Close-up of detailed dress

Hairstyles of the Rich 'n' Famous

Well, more like hairstyles for Damsels in the dungeons peelin' potatoes! I have roughed out a few sketches for possible hairdos for your Damsels in Distress characters. Try and apply these to your own designs as well.

The black lines that you see following the curve of the hair are invisible lines that I try and find when creating hair. Unless the hair is straight, try and use this technique. It will make the hair that you draw more pleasing to the eye.

The directional lines are what I visualize and draw when creating hair.

Deckhand Leonard

After leaving home and stowing away on Blackbeard's ship, Leonard is well accustomed to the needs and wants of his fellow pirate buddies. Given that Leo has no experience whatsoever in pillaging and pirating, he is resigned to the fact that he will be scrubbin' decks until he can prove himself a pirate.

Step One
The Face

Begin with a rough circle/sphere for his face. Then add in the guide lines for the eyes, nose and mouth.

Step Two
Face Details

The ears can now be drawn in. If you find it easier, start with an oval first, then mold them into ears once you are happy with the placement. The eyes will sit in line with the ears.

Eyes sit 'ere

Line your ears up with your eyes

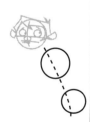

Construction of the Ear Close-Up

I will start with an oval or circle, placing it on the guide line. When you are happy with where it is, move on to step #2 and draw in the detail.

Step #1   Step #2

Step Three
The Torso

Before you go and slap on some clothes, think about the shapes that are used to create the torso. Also, think about the angle of the torso and what Leo is actually doing in movement. I have him slightly tilted, which reflects in the shapes I have constructed. So get in there and draw two ovals with the center line overlapping them.

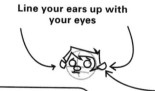

Think "ANGLES"

Why is Leo tilted? And no, he is not drunk!

Draw the mop on an angle 'cause it just looks better!

The shoulders

Draw the hands first

Arm bones

Step Four
Arms 'n' Legs and the Mop

I have drawn in two circles indicating where the shoulders sit so to help me place the arms in the correct place. Another trick that I use is drawing the basic shapes for the hands BEFORE I draw the bones of the arms. This way I can play around with different locations and see what works best. You can use this method with the feet as well. Once you have positioned the hands and feet correctly, draw in the bones for the arms and legs. The mop handle and head can be added last.

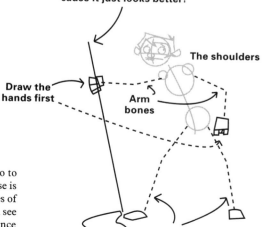

Are they ants or bones?

Step Five

Tubes and Stuff for the Arms 'n' Legs

Without fail, every time I draw HUMAN-style characters, TUBES will always be sketched in first. It just makes so much sense to add them in, mainly because if you are constructing something from scratch or you are sitting in front a group of friends or even a client, having the knowledge to draw a tube is invaluable! It will help you to visualize your character in an unlimited amount of poses and impress the socks off anyone watching!

Step-by-step breakdown of drawing the shirt and vest

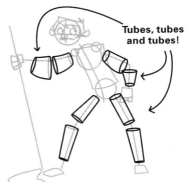

Tubes, tubes and tubes!

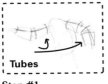

Tubes

Step #1

Create the arms and torso with shapes.

Shirt fabric

Vest

Step #2

The shirt fabric will follow the shape of the tubes you have drawn. The vest will then follow the shape of the shirt.

Collars

Step #3

The collar will need to go in now. Start from the center line.

Step Six

Bucket Full of Slop

The bucket is constructed with a simple tube shape with the handle looping through Leo's hand. Tilt the bucket toward the reader, so you can see what's inside. Try tilting the bucket on several angles and see what you come up with.

Leo's bucket of slop

Tilting toward you

Tilting away

Tilt toward you

This is the open end

Deckhand Leonard's Breakdown

Well, here is my construction of Deckhand Leonard. See how I get the angles correct on the arms, legs and mop handle before I go and add the detail.

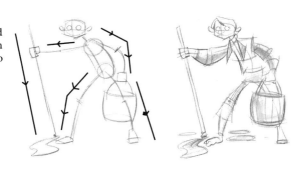

Facial Expressions

It's always a good skill to be able to draw different expressions on your character's face. The trick here is to use the same template for the face on all expressions. So using the one that I have drawn, all you need to do is change the eyes and the mouth.

Use this face template

Surprised	Cunning	Worried	Angry	Happy
"What the??..."	"I got a plan..."	"I lost me underwear..."	"You clean the toilet..."	"Did someone say 'beer'?..."

Makin' yer clothes look ye olde
(Translation: Making your clothes look old)

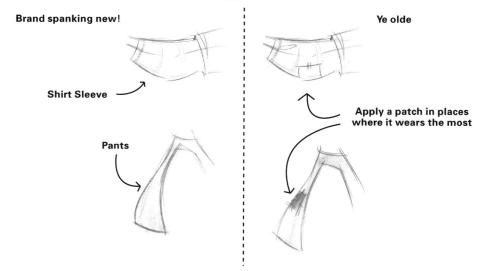

Brand spanking new!

Ye olde

Shirt Sleeve →

Pants →

Apply a patch in places where it wears the most

Patches You Can Use

Tip: Make the patches darker than the material you are applying them to. Also, place the stitches in random locations as Leonard is not very good at sewing.

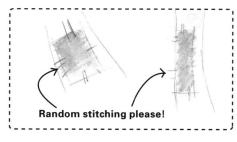

Random stitching please!

Dog

Busted again! Don't leave those bones lyin' around and don't leave your meal unattended, 'cause it won't be there when you get back!

This tutorial will show you a few tricks on how a dog or any other animal can have a bone lodged in its mouth. Have you ever wondered how to get teeth wrapped around a bone? Follow the next few steps and you will find out. I like his expression and pose, as he knows that he has done something bad and he thinks that he has gotten away with it! Always think about what sort of mood your character is in before you start to draw.

Step One

As with most characters I draw, I always start with an easy basic shape such as a circle to get the ball rolling. Add in those guide lines for the eyes and the center of the head. I have gone a bit horizontal on the nose guide, but this should help when drawing it in later. The solid line under the nose guide will be the start of the mouth. Lastly, add in the lines for the big floppy ears.

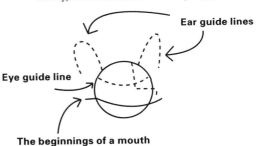

Ear guide lines

Eye guide line

The beginnings of a mouth

Step Two
Rest of His Facial Features

I have grayed out the previous step to make it a lot easier to figure out the next step. You can start by drawing in those "I haven't done anything so why are you looking at me?" eyes. Make sure they sit on the guide line. You can begin the nose with an oval and then CHISEL it out like a bit of wood until your nose looks like the dog's. Draw in his jaw and teeth. Lastly, sketch in two triangles for the ears. They can be molded later.

Raising the eyebrows makes the character look INTERESTED

Step Three
The Bone

The main thing to remember when drawing the bone (you can apply this principle to other drawings as well) is to draw the whole object rather than just the front or the end. The key is to draw it light so when you are happy with what you have drawn, you can go ahead and darken the appropriate lines.

Draw the complete bone

Step Four
The Torso

We will start the torso with two major circles roughly the same size. At the same time, sketch in the center line to help us point the dog in the right direction. This will also help the dog, as he can be a bit stupid sometimes and is going to need all the help he can get! Now draw in his guide lines for the arms, legs and tail.

Step Five
Arms 'n' Legs

Having sketched in the guide lines for the doggy limbs, we can quite safely add the tubes to give them MASS. Knowing how to draw TUBES confidently will help you to draw from your mind a lot easier.

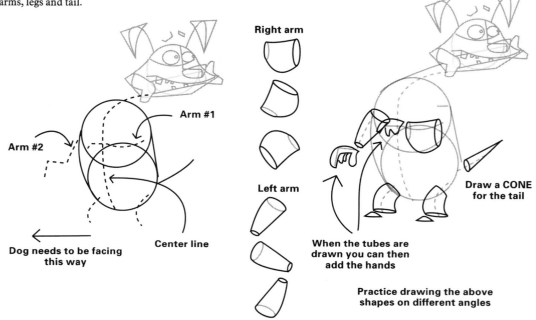

Right arm

Arm #1

Arm #2

Left arm

Center line

Dog needs to be facing this way

Draw a **CONE** for the tail

When the tubes are drawn you can then add the hands

Practice drawing the above shapes on different angles

The Final Breakdown

Do you understand how the dog has been constructed? Try drawing the dog now without looking at my tutorial and see what you can remember. Notice how I didn't draw too much detail in the first sketch as I just wanted to get everything in the right place. In my rough breakdowns, I will tend to smudge my linework to get some volume happening. This lets me know whether I am on track to drawing a great looking picture.

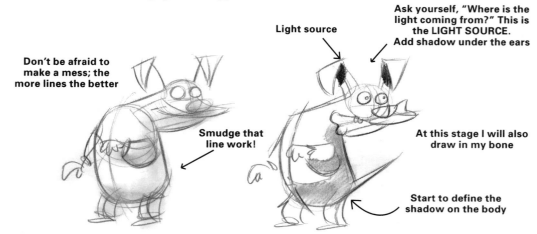

Don't be afraid to make a mess; the more lines the better

Smudge that line work!

Light source

Ask yourself, "Where is the light coming from?" This is the LIGHT SOURCE. Add shadow under the ears

At this stage I will also draw in my bone

Start to define the shadow on the body

A Wee Bit Extra

The Bone

The dog's bone is made up of a few easy shapes
and can be completed in three easy steps.

Step #1	Step #2	Step #3
	No, they are not eggs!	**Define the outline**

 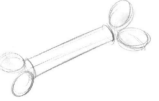 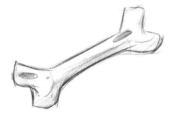

Draw a line with half ovals on each end.

Over the top of those guide lines draw in a tube for the main part and two ovals on both ends.

Define the outline until it looks like bone shown above.

Texture: a small oval can indicate texture on an object

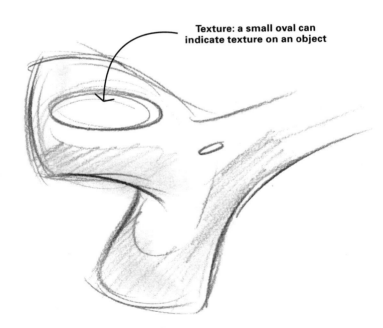

Here is a close-up of the end of the bone. Add a few ovals on the surface to give it some texture. Rub your finger over the shadowed parts to give the bone a nice airbrushed look.

The Monkey, aka Rodriguez

It seems that we have caught Rodriguez in an awkward position. If you don't look at him directly, he will presume that you haven't seen him and will continue rummaging through the food quarters on the ship.

The Breakdown

The main idea behind drawing Rodriguez was to have him flying through the air with his big monkey hands flopping all over the place. The bananas added an extra element to the picture to make it more interesting. Keep an eye out for those big goofy hands and make sure that they look identical to the feet!

Step One
The Face

Okay, let's start with drawing a light, rough circle for the head. Next we will add some guide lines to help us place the facial features, such as the eyes and mouth.

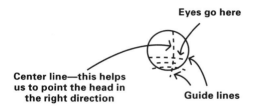

Eyes go here

Center line—this helps us to point the head in the right direction

Guide lines

Step Two
Facial Features

Don't let Rodriguez know that we are giving him a goofy look. He sees himself more as a cheeky four-legged runaway. A goofy look can be created by drawing wide eyes with the pupils looking aimlessly toward nothing in particular. Draw the ears as ovals first and then adjust accordingly. The nostrils can now be placed in their correct place, and the shape of the mouth can be drawn in.

Tip: On the main drawing you will notice the right eye is smaller with the eyebrow squashing the eye down. Instead of having two parts of the face identical, try doing what I did. This will create some interest in his expression.

Use ovals for the ears and don't forget to make 'em hairy

Bring eyebrow down

Step Three
Torso

The torso can be drawn before step two if you like. This will depend on how you draw and personal preference. The torso helps keep the rest of the body well proportioned.

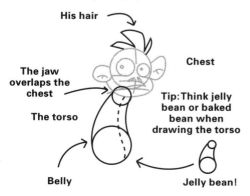

His hair

Chest

The jaw overlaps the chest

The torso

Tip: Think jelly bean or baked bean when drawing the torso

Belly

Jelly bean!

Step Four
Arms 'n' Legs

Rodriguez considers himself to be quite the versatile mammal, utilizing his feet as hands and his hands as feet. Attached to these are his arms and legs. Before you run off and start drawing all the cool stuff for the arms and legs, think about his bones first. These are represented by the dashed lines. Sketch them out in a fluid, natural motion, starting from the torso and moving outward.

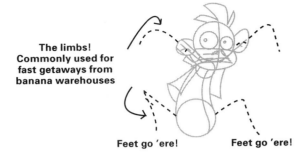

The limbs! Commonly used for fast getaways from banana warehouses

Feet go 'ere!   **Feet go 'ere!**

Step Five
Hands and Feet

Now let's draw the hard stuff. I've begun drawing the hands with dotted outlines and have added directional lines to help you start the hands.

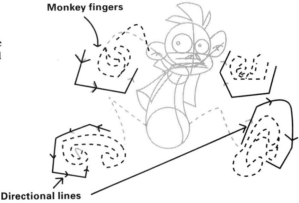

Monkey fingers

Directional lines

Step Six
Tubes

Another important shape to master is the TUBE. The TUBE will give your characters arms and legs a nice consistent size and will also add volume. Tubes help you to draw arms that can go backward or forward. This technique will help when you are drawing from your mind.

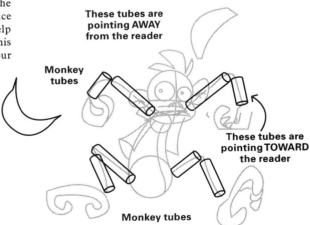

These tubes are pointing AWAY from the reader

Monkey tubes

These tubes are pointing TOWARD the reader

Monkey tubes

My Final Breakdown

This is how I will break down Rodriguez once my shapes are in the right place. Just remember not to draw the construction lines too dark at this stage as you are still feeling your way through the character and may need to change a few things later.

Phase One

Create FLUID construction lines for the arms and legs. Use this time to get a better feel for his pose. I will use strong angles to create a strong dynamic character. See how I started the hands? They look quite similar to hooks.

Phase Two

Now I am starting to flesh out the anatomy of the character by adding in some major details and getting a good feeling about where everything will sit. KEEP IT LIGHT!

The final rendering in Photoshop

The Parrot

Where do I start? This parrot is a bit of a talker and quite intelligent, some might say. He'll observe your every move and pass that intimate knowledge on to people who want it, so be careful with what you do and say around him!

The Parrot Breakdown

This outline shows the shape I used to begin sketching the wings. It's vital that you draw the outline to give yourself boundaries to work within.

Sketch the wings with a boundary first

Step One
The Torso

Rather than starting with the head, this time I will start with the torso and describe in detail how to draw the head at the end of the tutorial. So, let's begin with the three major torso shapes: the head, chest and torso. Draw circles and lay them over the LINE OF ACTION. These are to be drawn lightly since we don't want to see them when the drawing is finished. The line of action is important as it keeps the character on the correct angle.

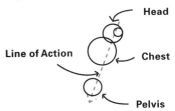

Step Two
Nose 'n' Feet

I have now added a center line to help me find the middle of the parrot and two lines on either side of the circles to give myself the torso. Chuck the beak on the head and make sure it's sitting on the right-hand side of the guide line. Draw in the guide lines for the legs and finish off with the feet/claws/talons.

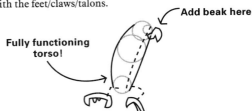

Step Three
Starting the Wings

The main thing to look for when beginning the wings will be the bones/arms, as indicated here. This will give us a starting point to add the rest of the detail.

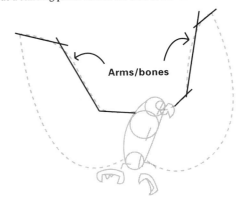

Step Four
Wings

Before going ahead and drawing in all the feathers and makin' him look pretty, I will explain how you can draw perfect wings. First, squint your eyes and visualize the OUTLINE of the wings (see my drawing). Then, very lightly sketch in this outline and don't forget the tail, otherwise he will just fly around in circles all day!

Sketch this outline

These are GUIDE lines so keep 'em light!

Step Five
Feathers

I ain't going to lie on this one: drawing feathers can be a tough task even for the most accomplished artist, so it's going to take some practice. If you can, take a look on the Internet for bird feathers and then practice drawing them in live action. Once you have had a go, come back here to finish the bird.

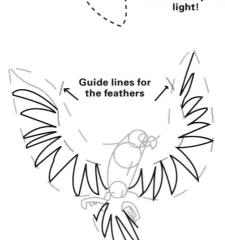

Guide lines for the feathers

When applying the feathers, very lightly draw in a guide line so they have a place to start and finish

The Breakdown

Here you see the transition from SHAPES to detail. See how light my pencil work is, which helps me in the end as I have fewer lines to rub out.

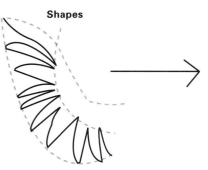

Shapes

Draft render

Tip: When it comes to the detail, SLOW down and really observe what you are drawing. When you get into rendering mode, sit back and take a look regularly. See where you have gone wrong and adjust accordingly.

Step Five
The Head Breakdown

Step #1

Let's see how I began drawing the parrot's head. Begin with a well-drawn sphere and add the guide line so the eye can sit on it.

Step #2

Draw another smaller sphere for the eye.

Step #3

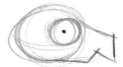

Continue on and add the beak, but keep it simple for now.

Step #4

Start to add some more detail, such as the lines under his eye, and begin to curve the beak a little.

Step #5

Now start the final touch up using the rubbing technique. Think about where the light is coming from, because this will give the character some depth.

Pirate Mate #1

This is one of Blackbeard's hired goons, who will serve and protect until there is nothing to serve and protect...or until a mutiny, whichever comes first.

Step One
The Face

Begin with a rough circle/sphere for his face. Then add in the guide lines for the eyes, nose and mouth. Add the jaw next, which is the shape of a rectangle, and place this on an angle.

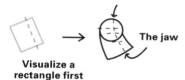

Center line

The jaw

Visualize a rectangle first

Step Two
Face Details

Now that we have the guides in their correct places, draw in the eyes, ears and nose. The nose will always overlap the center guide line. Draw in the hat next, with the hair growing out of it.

Use the guide lines to place the eyes

Step Three
The Torso

I have decided to use 3D blocks to construct Mate #1's torso (refer back to the perspective tutorials at the beginning of the book). Since the character is turned, we are going to see one side and not the other. This will apply to both the chest and the pelvis. The center line will be closer to the far side as well.

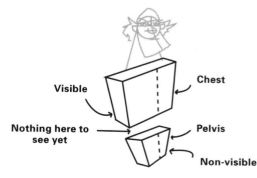

Visible

Chest

Nothing here to see yet

Pelvis

Non-visible

Step Four
Arms 'n' legs

This is the type of pose that has FORESHORTENING applied to it. Foreshortening is where you have objects, in this case limbs, coming toward you or going away. Look at the lower right leg and you may notice that it is getting smaller, hence the smaller guide line. You will see in the next step how I use tubes to achieve this effect. Start with two circles to indicate where the shoulders start, then lightly sketch in the guide lines (bones) for the arms. Apply this technique to the legs as well.

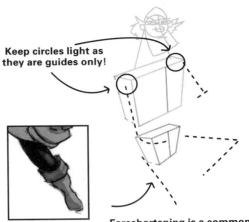

Keep circles light as they are guides only!

Foreshortening is a common technique used in many styles of art, such as action comics

Step Five
Tubes 'n' Stuff

Okay, you are going to have some weird looking tubes sketched in on the body for this step. Take a look at the way I drew the right arm and notice how thick it is. This doesn't mean he has an arm the size of a small tree, as I am following the shape of his shirt. Same goes with his left arm. If you look carefully at his left arm, you will notice that the bottom half has two overlapping circles. This technique helps me to draw the arm coming toward me. This is also the same with the right leg, except it is going away from me. So go ahead and draw in the tubes for both the arms and legs, making sure you use your guide line to help with the direction and angles.

Left arm

Overlapping circles

Right arm

Use the guide lines for direction

Right leg

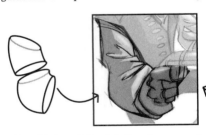

No, this is not Captain Tree Arm man. I drew the shape of the shirt in the form of two tubes, then transformed them into a short sleeve

Step Six
Hands 'n' Guns (and a Wee Bit of Smoke)

Let's start with the LEFT hand and how it's constructed. I will begin by drawing in a 3D box that will overlap the forearm we drew in the previous step. Then, very carefully, draw a tube for each finger. Notice how the two middle fingers are touching. This is a little trick that illustrators use to make the hand more interesting to look at. Lastly, sketch in another tube for the thumb. The right hand is started with a box as well. You may need to practice this one on another piece of paper to get it right! The gun barrel is drawn next and, as you can see, it's a basic tube shape. The smoke is lightly sketched in with the SIDE of your pencil to get a nice airbrushed, smoky look.

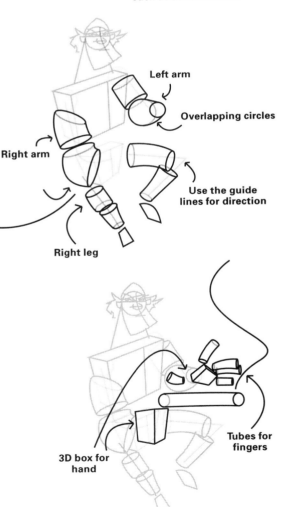

Tubes for fingers

3D box for hand

More Rough Drawings

When developing a character, I generally sketch a lot before deciding on what pose I want to use. Once I have a good idea the next step is to clean up the picture as shown below.

Phase One
Basic Shapes

Creating with simple shapes

Keeping it light

Imagine seeing these tubes here!

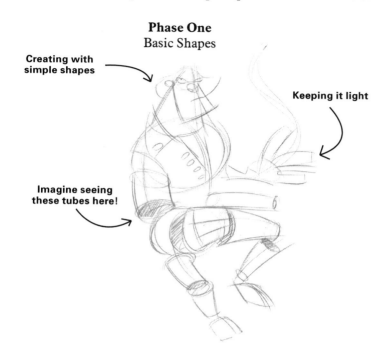

Phase Two
Detailed Rough

Practicing hands

May have been a foot? Who knows...

Female Pirate

Finding a female pirate these days is rare, but when you do manage to spot one be very aware of your gold! Her beauty is deceptive, which allows her to get close to her victims and take whatever she wants. Unlike male pirates, female pirates do wash and will occasionally even sail into port to get a pirate manicure.

Female Pirate Breakdown

Females in general tend to be smaller, with smaller chests and legs, etc. In this pose she will be flying through the air to pillage another ship.

Step One
The Head

Okay, let's get into it, since this pirate has got some pillaging to do. Let's start with drawing a light, rough circle, as this gives us a great place to start drawing the rest of the body. Just below the circle add the jaw line; we draw this separately because it is a movable part. The dotted lines that you can see are construction lines that act as guides, so later on we can add the facial features like the nose and mouth. Next sketch in the spine.

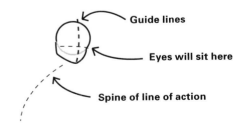

Guide lines

Eyes will sit here

Spine of line of action

Step Two
The Hair

Female pirates always worry about their hair, so try not to make it too boyish or it will most likely be the last thing that you draw! You can now add the hat over the top of the hair.

Tip: Try drawing the outline of the hair first, as shown below. Then once you have done that, finish the strands of hair that are on the inside.

You can now add the facial features such as the eyes, nose and mouth, using the guide lines we drew earlier.

Still keeping it light

Draw the outline of the hair if you are not sure

Step Three
The Torso and Limbs

Now, in order to add the arms and legs we will need the torso to be drawn in. This will help us place the limbs. Think of the chest and pelvis area as two movable parts, and draw them in as circles as shown in this step. Connect them together with two curved lines.

Tip: Make sure that the chest and pelvis shapes are smaller than the shape of the head. In the cartoon world we call this PROPORTIONALLY CORRECT!

Once the torso had been drawn correctly you can add the arms and legs. But instead of drawing the whole lot in one go, we will start with light construction lines. That way we can see if they are in the correct place before we add the detail.

Step Four
Hands and Feet

It's time we added the hands and feet, otherwise she won't be going very far. For the feet you can start with rounded triangle shapes and then mold them into boots. For the hands I would start with a rough circle to make sure they are placed in the correct area, then finish off with the fingers. Don't draw the circles dark as they are only there to help place the hands and keep them the correct size.

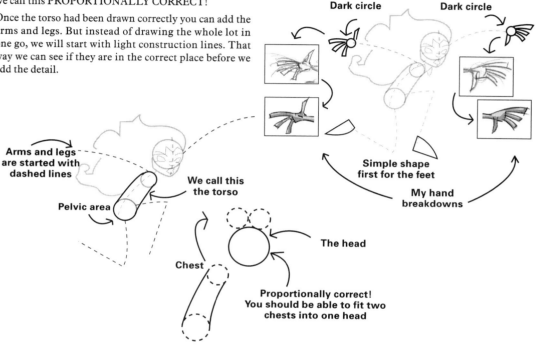

Dark circle   **Dark circle**

Simple shape first for the feet

My hand breakdowns

Arms and legs are started with dashed lines

Pelvic area

We call this the torso

Chest

The head

Proportionally correct! You should be able to fit two chests into one head

Step Five
Legs 'n' Arms

Now that we have created some guide lines for the arms, we can quite safely draw in some tubes for the arms and legs. I draw two tubes each for arms and legs because where these two tubes meet will be a rotational point.

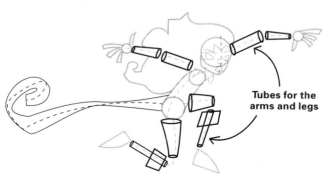

Tubes for the arms and legs

My Final Breakdown
This is my damsel from start to finish. Remember to start light.

Phase One

Phase Two

My finished rendering

Chapter 4
Pirate Enemies

Cannibal

Whatever you do, don't get stranded on an island with this man. As you can see, he has a rather large sword and skulls which hang from his neck... If you do manage to find yourself on an island with this fella, it's probably a safe bet that you will be asked to dinner that night.

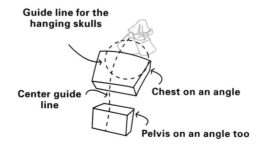

Cannibal Breakdown

In this drawing you have to emphasize the fact that he likes to munch on the occasional human, so I thought the skulls showed just that. If you like, think of other parts of the body you could hang off his neck and draw them also!

Step One
The Face

Begin with a rough circle/sphere for his face. Then add in the guide lines for the eyes, nose and mouth. This is another face that starts on an angle, so keep this in mind.

Construction lines

Keep face on angle

Step Two
The Bowl Haircut

Now I know they don't have a barber to cut the lads' hair, so I'm guessin' they would grab the nearest coconut, crack it in half and use it to get a nice clean cut. Notice how the hair has a gap from the skull.

What size coconut was that?

The ears

Step Three
A Big Neck

Try and visualize a tube for his neck; if it's a bit tricky, draw it in as a flat shape.

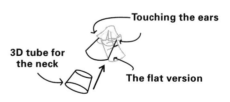

Touching the ears

3D tube for the neck

The flat version

Step Four
Cannibal Torso

Now, after eating all the spare humans on the island, our cannibal man has found himself with a big chest (must be all the protein!). So now draw in two 3D boxes, one for the chest and the other for the pelvis. You will also notice that I have drawn a circle over the chest. This will be where the skulls hang, just remember to sketch it in lightly.

Guide line for the hanging skulls

Center guide line

Chest on an angle

Pelvis on an angle too

Step Five
Arms 'n' Legs

The key to getting your arms and legs in the correct place is to draw in the bones first; these bones are represented by the dashed lines on the character. I draw these in first to get a good idea of what it will look like before I go ahead and add the detail. Block out the hands and feet and also make sure the hands are positioned in the correct place. The left hand is in line with the pelvis. Notice what the back foot is in line with.

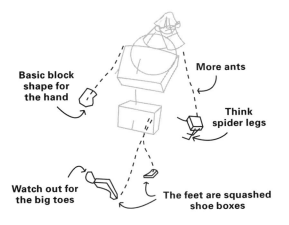

Basic block shape for the hand

More ants

Think spider legs

Watch out for the big toes

The feet are squashed shoe boxes

Step Six
More Arms and More Legs

Now that you know that the arms will be in the correct place you will need to add the bulk/mass of the arms. The best way to approach this is with tubes. You can start with a basic shape or, if you are having a great day with the pencil, try molding the tube into more of a bicep or forearm like what I have done. The back hind leg will be difficult to draw, so study the small tutorial and see how I created it.

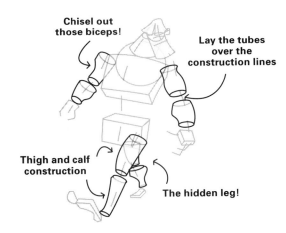

Chisel out those biceps!

Lay the tubes over the construction lines

Thigh and calf construction

The hidden leg!

Step by Step Guide to Drawing the Legs

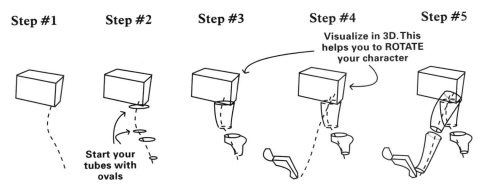

Step #1   **Step #2**   **Step #3**   **Step #4**   **Step #5**

Visualize in 3D. This helps you to ROTATE your character

Start your tubes with ovals

Step Seven
The Mighty Knife and Skulls

This part of the drawing is where I had the most fun. I mean, who doesn't like drawing skulls!? Let's begin with drawing five circles over the guide I created earlier. Don't worry if it's not exact, just as long as they fit in there comfortably. Now notice how the skull hanging off his body is in midair. I have drawn it this way to indicate that the character is in full motion, and the skull is actually bouncing off his thigh as he moves. Lastly, draw the knife in, making sure that the TIP of the knife is close to the big toe.

Place skulls here

Big croc knife

Place another skull here

Sketches of Cannibal

This is quite a hard image to draw since there is so much happening here. He's looking over his shoulder with his neck twisted, both his arms and legs are doing the opposite of each other, PLUS he's holding that huge crocodile knife! Oh yeah, and don't forget the moving skull that bounces off his thigh.

Keep it loose and light!

This should be your next level of detail

Drawing the tattoos on the cannibal

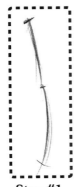

Step #1
Begin with guide lines for the arms.

Step #2
Block in the shapes using tubes.

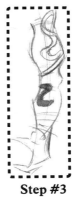

Step #3
Sketch in the outlines of the tattoos, then shade in the ink last.

Step #4
Color your arm!

Tattoo Close-up

Cannibals might have all kinds of tattoos etched on their skin, like snakes, skulls, their wife (or wives) or warrior symbols like a picture of them throwing a spear.

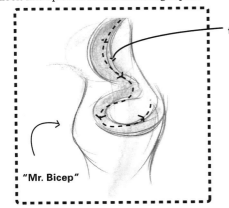

Tattoo pattern— follow the drawn line

"Mr. Bicep"

The Man Skirt

(No laughing, otherwise you will be invited to dinner.)

Step #1
Block out the main shapes for the torso and pelvic area.

Step #2
Sketch in the basic shape for where the Man Skirt will be hanging.

Step #3
Add the grass-like substance with downward strokes; take note of how the grass curves around the thigh.

Step #4
Add the color.

Skulls

I thought I would draw some sketches of the skulls that are resting on the cannibal's chest.

Step #1

Begin with a rough circle and guide lines.

Step #2

Add the cheekbones.

Step #3

Sketch in the jaw.

Step #4

Add the teeth and eyes.

Rough Sketch of the Skulls

This was one of initial sketches of the skulls hanging from the cannibal's neck. I was quite happy with it, so I think one trace over should do the trick.

Royal Navy Captain

Step One
The Face

Begin with a rough circle/sphere for his face. Then add in the guide lines for the eyes, nose and mouth. Take note of his rather large jaw line.

Guide lines

Large jaw line

Step Three
Big Fluffy Hair and Torso

I'm not too sure what they were thinking when they were handing out wigs. I have drawn the basic shape here; just add the detail. The torso is made up of two circles joined together like a jelly bean.

Hey man, nice wig!

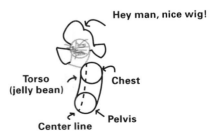

Torso (jelly bean)   **Chest**

Center line   **Pelvis**

Step Two
Eyes, Nose and Mouth

Draw over the guide lines with the main facial features: the eyes, nose and mouth.

Don't forget the scowling eyebrow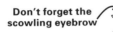

Step Four
Arms, Legs, Hands and the Gun

Sketch in the guide lines for the arms and legs, as this will help you achieve a more natural pose for your character. Notice how he is leaning back a bit. This is because he is moving in midair and is in the middle of an action. Keep the gun a simple shape for now and add the detail later.

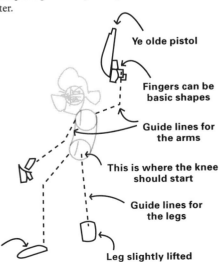

Ye olde pistol

Fingers can be basic shapes

Guide lines for the arms

This is where the knee should start

Guide lines for the legs

Leg slightly lifted

If you did not know, this is the RIGHT foot

Step Five
Tubes for the Arms

Happy with where the guide lines are? Then go ahead and draw in the tubes to give the arms a nice solid mass.

Step Six
Tubes for the Legs

This is quite an interesting pose. You will notice that the left leg is considerably shorter than the right. This is because he has it lifted with the THIGH pointing straight at us. This is called FORESHORTENING. It's indicated as a circle just above the calf muscle.

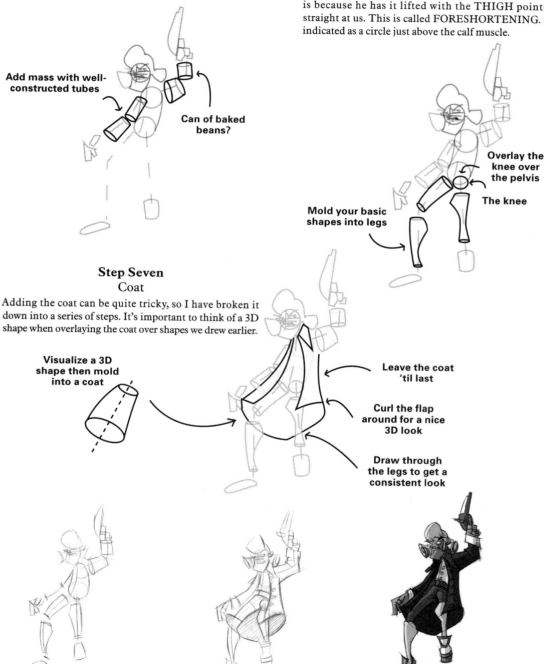

Add mass with well-constructed tubes

Can of baked beans?

Overlay the knee over the pelvis

The knee

Mold your basic shapes into legs

Step Seven
Coat

Adding the coat can be quite tricky, so I have broken it down into a series of steps. It's important to think of a 3D shape when overlaying the coat over shapes we drew earlier.

Visualize a 3D shape then mold into a coat

Leave the coat 'til last

Curl the flap around for a nice 3D look

Draw through the legs to get a consistent look

Three-step breakdown

The Royal Navy Lieutenants

Every captain needs a lieutenant, so here are three for you to practice drawing.

One of Many Magpies...

Magpies are devious creatures who suit the pirate life well. Make sure you don't have any shiny things near your face or you may find yourself a walking target on the ship.

Magpie Breakdown

I was going to draw a magpie flying but decided to give it life with a more cartoonish pose. You would never actually see a magpie pointing at something, but if you allow yourself to stretch the imagination a bit you will be one step closer to becoming a character designer.

Step Two
Eyeball and the Neck

Since we have the guide line in the correct place, you will feel more comfortable in placing the eye. Keep it light for now. The neck can be a 3D tube—take note of its angle. Remember that all the lines we are drawing now are meant to be light, since we will not be using all of them later.

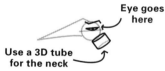

Eye goes here

Use a 3D tube for the neck

Step Four
Bird feet

Here's an easy one for you. Draw some guide lines (bones) coming from the stomach. Then add the bones of the feet. You can also add the main bulk of the feet as well.

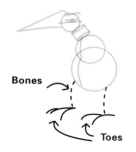

Bones

Toes

Step One
The Beak

This character is a little bit different from most of the others I have created because it features a SIDE profile. Start with a circle, then add a triangular shape for the beak. Add the guide line for the eye.

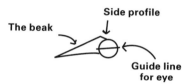

Side profile

The beak

Guide line for eye

Step Three
The Torso

The magpie has a nice pear-shaped, jelly bean body. The most likely cause of this fatness is all the excessive drinking and eating he does with the captain. Sketch in two circles and have them overlapping. Take note of the stomach shape, as it is a lot bigger than the chest. Now add the center line and keep it to the left side of the torso. The center line is a handy resource as we can automatically tell which way the character is facing.

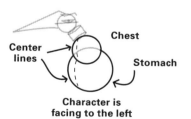

Chest

Center lines

Stomach

Character is facing to the left

Legs and feather breakdown

Step #1 Begin with the shape shown.

Step #2 Add in a basic rectangular shape for where the feathers will sit. Add more bone for the feet.

Step #3 Very roughly sketch in random lines to represent the feathers.

Step Five
Left Wing and Feather Legs

The left wing is not doing much in this drawing, so it needs to look nice just sitting there. We can add the feathers a little later on. The legs have small feathers protruding from the base of the stomach, so take a look at the side note on how I did the feathers.

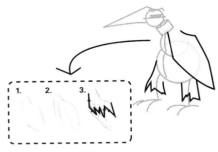

Wing Breakdown

Step #1 Start with the basic shape as shown.

Step #2 Add each feather individually.

Step #3 Split the wing with diagonal lines as shown.

Step Six
The Right Wing and Tail

This will be a little tricky, since the magpie is actually telling someone what to do! The trick to drawing a wing that is outstretched is to break it down into a really simple shape. Sketch it in lightly, then stand back and squint your eyes, looking at both the original and half-constructed drawings. Does everything look proportionally correct? If not, adjust and repeat the process. I have added human-style fingers on the end of the wing to make the drawing more interesting. The tail can be added on last. Draw it in a way that indicates it is lying on the ground.

Wing breakdown

Step #1 Draw a horizontal line.

Step #2 Draw a line to represent the underneath of the wing.

Step #3 Add each feather individually (see dark lines).

Pencil sketch breakdown - look for FLOW patterns

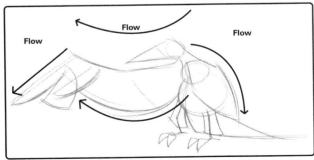

Keep your lines light and rough, use lots of fluid line motions and look for areas with FLOW

What is FLOW?

Flow is a technique that can make your drawings natural and fluid-like. I use this method in all of my drawings to keep them consistently looking great. Look at the arrows and which way they move. With your pencil in hand and using a large A3 sheet of paper move your WHOLE arm in a sweeping arc motion from the shoulder and practice the flow lines as shown. Tip: Draw BIG! Use the whole sheet of paper and don't draw from the wrist—draw from the shoulder.

Sea Monster

Lurking in the depths is "Sea Monster." Until recently, this beast of the ocean has been floating around near the sea floor, dining on the delights of scaly fish things and fish bugs.

Step One
The Face

Being a sea monster, it won't have the conventional face structure of a human, but in this drawing I have tried to keep it simple. Begin as you normally do with heads, by drawing in the circle with guide lines for the eyes and mouth.

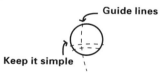

Guide lines

Keep it simple

Step Two
Facial Features and Chest

Lay the eyes on top of the guide line and place the eyebrows just above them as shown. Draw in the mouth carefully. Take note of where the mouth starts and finishes. Just below the circle, sketch in an oval for the chest. Well, to be quite honest I don't know if it does have a chest, but draw it in anyway to give the torso some mass.

Banana eyebrows

Note where the mouth starts

Chest

Step Three
The Beginnings of the Squid-like Arms

Hey look! It's a bunch of lost ants... It's always a good idea to sketch in a few rough lines to help place the tentacles in the best place. You can also draw the horns. Notice how I CURL the end of the tentacles.

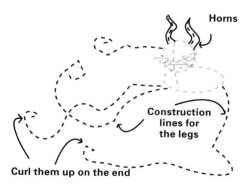

Horns

Construction lines for the legs

Curl them up on the end

Step Four
Chunking Out Those Tentacles

Using the sphere and oval as your starting points, sketch in the tubes to indicate mass and direction. You can start with simple tube shapes if you like then mold them into the shape of the tentacle. Keep looking back at my drawing for reference so your drawing will be accurate.

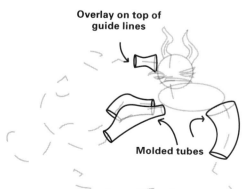

Overlay on top of guide lines

Molded tubes

Step Five
More Chunking and the Bits Underneath

Using the guide lines we drew earlier, overlay the rest of the tubes carefully. You will start to see the tentacles appearing in front of you. For the slimy bits underneath, draw six random, curvy lines to indicate that the tentacles would be swirling around in water.

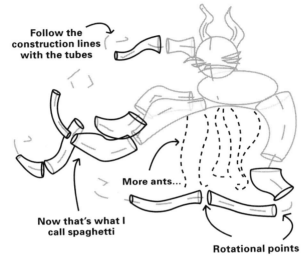

Follow the construction lines with the tubes

More ants...

Now that's what I call spaghetti

Rotational points

Step Six
Finalizing the Tentacles and Boat

If you look at where the sky and sea meet, the line that appears is the HORIZON line. Here, you will notice the boat sitting on that line. The boat is constructed from a 3D block. Finish the tentacles underneath the monster by adding some thickness over the guide lines. And last but not least, don't forget to draw the little fish, which is indicated by the small circle hovering around underneath the sea monster.

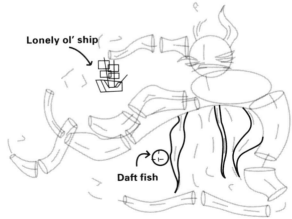

Lonely ol' ship

Daft fish

More tentacles

Drawing Tentacles

If you can visualize tentacles as winding tubes, then you are pretty much halfway to finishing them. When adding the suckers (the round parts), start with one circle first and randomly spread it along one side of the tentacle. When you are happy with the placement of this first circle, repeat it again but with a slightly smaller circle. Do this three times with three different circles. Make sure that the beginning of the tentacle is big and taper it off when you get to the end.

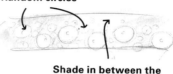

Big at this end

Keep suckers to one side as much as you can

Tapered off here

Random circles

Shade in between the circles for a nice effect

Joining the Tentacles

The best approach for joining tentacles is to visualize them as 3D shapes and think about the connection point where the shapes will meet. Are they the same shape and size? Do they connect correctly?

This is the torso of the sea monster (it's just broken down into shapes)

Keep both ends the same shape

Think construction blocks

Follow the arrows

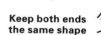

Sea Monster In Construction Mode
In order to make your drawing natural and fluid, it's always a good idea to plan where your shapes are going to sit before attempting any detail.

Rough #1

Rough #2

Shadows will make a drawing interesting to the eye

Near the end of the sketch, look a little closer at what you are drawing. Begin thinking about shadows and how they look when hitting the skin of the sea monster. Ask yourself, "Would the shadow hit this part of the body?"

Ye Olde Skeleton

Lost a skeleton anyone? Where do bad pirates go when they have sunk to the depths of the sea? They go to Skeleton Hell! This old skeleton has been lurking in the real world for a while now, usually attacking anything that has a heartbeat.

Step One
The Face

Begin by drawing a circle and laying down the guide lines to indicate where the eyes, nostrils and mouth are. From the eye line draw in the jaw and keep it nice and square.

Start the jaw here

Indicates the skull

Keep it square

Step Two
Facial Features and Back Bone

Using the guide lines, draw in the two eyes. Then very lightly sketch in the neck and backbone. We will need these to help place the chest.

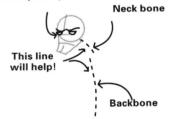

Place your eyes here

Neck bone

This line will help!

Backbone

Step Three
Basic Shapes for the Chest and Pelvis

I would class the skeleton as a "human-style drawing" even though it ain't human! It's a general rule that I apply when the physique of a character is human-like. So the main shapes used in a human-style drawing would be the 3D chest and pelvis as shown below. Check out the perspective section on how to get dynamic shapes such as these.

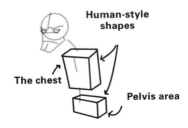

Human-style shapes

The chest

Pelvis area

Step Four
Guide Lines for the Arms 'n' Legs

The guide lines seen here should be drawn lightly as they are there to help place the rest of the limbs. If you draw them too dark, it will just make the drawing way too messy! I have placed in a few basic shapes for the hands and feet, just so I know where I should put the detail later on.

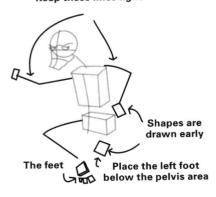

Keep these lines light

Shapes are drawn early

The feet

Place the left foot below the pelvis area

Step Five
Toes, Fingers and a Sword

We'll begin with the right hand. The key here is to draw the fingers as bones, which is not as hard as it looks. Just copy my technique with basic block shapes, then later on you can mold them into bones. Draw in a blockish shape for the left arm's elbow bone and the right leg's knee. The toes can be added by just drawing in small block shapes as shown. The sword's blade starts off with a guide line, but keep this light as it will not be shown in the drawing.

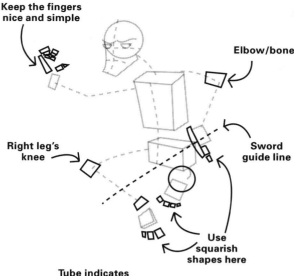

Keep the fingers nice and simple

Elbow/bone

Right leg's knee

Sword guide line

Use squarish shapes here

Step Six
Tubes and More Sword Parts

We have come to the last step in creating a zombie skeleton. The big tubes you see here represent the clothes. Take note of how the sleeves are not in line with each other, as this will make the drawing more visually appealing to the viewer. The sword blade and handle can be added in now by using the guide line we drew earlier.

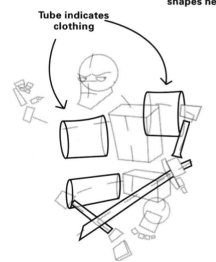

Tube indicates clothing

The Old Breakdown

In this breakdown I have visualized 3D shapes for the chest and pelvis area. I also use sweeping rough lines to help keep a consistent look throughout the construction process. As I near the end of the drawing, you can see I am getting a good feeling for the detail. Note that I am still sketching lightly.

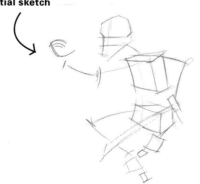

Initial sketch

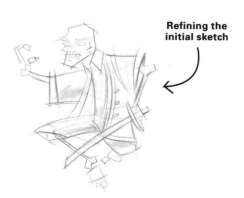

Refining the initial sketch

Some Extras to Practice With!

I had some rough concept expressions lying around the studio and thought it would be a good idea to add them here for you to practice with.

The "I ain't talking to you so I am going to look this way" look

The "Why am I here?" look

The "I am about to eat you" look

The "Did you hear that?" look

The "You eat my bananas, lad?" look

The "All right...who farted?" look

The "Did I forget to put my clothes on this morning?" look

Henry the Zombie Monkey

What pirate world would NOT have a zombie monkey? Unlike his living monkey counterpart, Henry is undead. This means he is stuck in the middle world, sailing the seas with other undead creatures and annoying the hell out of the living.

Breakdown of Henry the Zombie Monkey

I like the idea of monkeys in full motion, so when you draw Henry, be aware of his motion and surroundings.

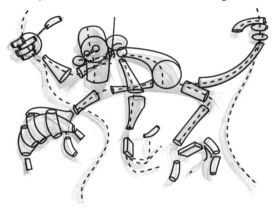

Step Two
Face Details

The next step can be quite tricky, so look on he following pages for some great tips and techniques! Place the eyes on the guide line with two small circles. When drawing the ears, take note that they are two different sizes and the right ear is significantly lower than the left.

Step One
The Face

This undead monkey has a big forehead, so I have added on an extra shape to compensate for it. As usual, draw in the guide lines that help place the eyes, nose and mouth.

Big left ear

Small right ear

Not in line with each other!

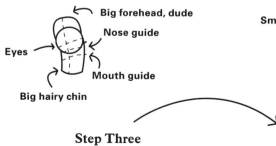

Big forehead, dude

Nose guide

Eyes

Mouth guide

Big hairy chin

Step Three
The Torso

Henry's torso is placed at a strange angle, so the first thing you will need to do is draw the center line. Then add the chest and pelvis circles. Take note of where the chest starts, as it is virtually overlapping the ear. The best way to place the chest accurately is to visualize how many pelvis circles you can fit between the head and pelvis.

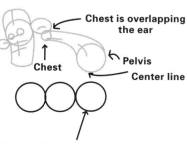

Chest is overlapping the ear

Chest

Pelvis

Center line

The head-to-pelvis area is two "pelvis" circles across

Step Four
Limbs, Vines and the Tail

In order to have your character hanging in a natural monkey pose, it's always a good idea to sketch in the arms and legs and any other moveable hanging objects very lightly. With this technique you can see if the pose is working for you or not. If it's not, then all you need to do is sketch some more lines in until it looks good. The best bit of advice I can pass on here is to think of angles when drawing. Look at the example to see what I mean.

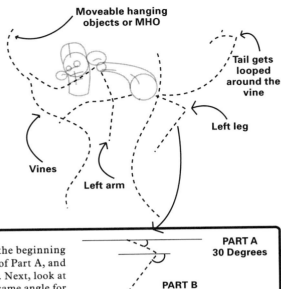

Moveable hanging objects or MHO

Tail gets looped around the vine

Left leg

Vines

Left arm

Imagine a horizontal line at the beginning of the leg. Look at the angle of Part A, and transfer that to your drawing. Next, look at the angle of Part B. Use that same angle for your drawing.

**PART A
30 Degrees**

**PART B
120 Degrees**

Step Five
Feet and Hands

This is another tricky step to perfect, so please take note of the small tips around the drawing to help you out. Starting with the right hand, draw a circle that will indicate where the palm is. The tail can now be brought into action. Have it looping around the vine. I used a couple of ovals to help me get the wraparound of the tail looking good. You can now draw in the feet, starting with a 3D box as the BASE and then adding your guide lines for the toes. Once you are happy with the placement, sketch in the tubes.

Step #1
Start with a circle.

Step #2
Draw a guide line coming off the circle then add a tube for the thumb.

Step #3
Finally, add four fingers across the face of the circle.

Right hand

Use ovals for the "wrap" around

Vine

Right foot help file

Use tubes for the fingers/toes

Step #1
Begin with the base of the foot.

Step #2
Sketch in the banana overlapping the foot.

Step #3
Now draw in the toes (like fingers), starting with tubes and then turning them into fingers later.

Step Six
Tubes for the Arms and Legs

How are we doing so far? This is a pretty complex drawing, so it may take you a couple of attempts to get it right. Try and visualize the tubes as 3D shapes rather than FLAT, 2D shapes. Thinking in 3D can make a drawing jump out and off the sheet of paper, while a 2D image will be flat and lifeless. You can start your tubes without any curves in them, and then when you are feeling confident with the placement you can go ahead and mold them into the correct shape.

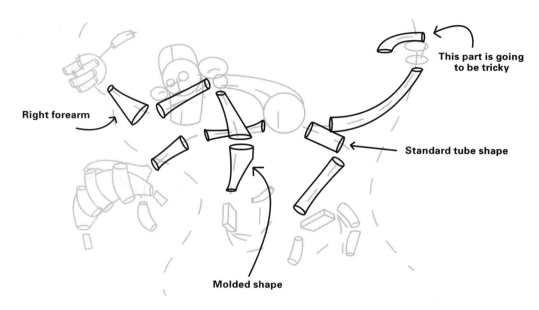

Right forearm

This part is going to be tricky

Standard tube shape

Molded shape

Extras

Here are some extras to practice with.

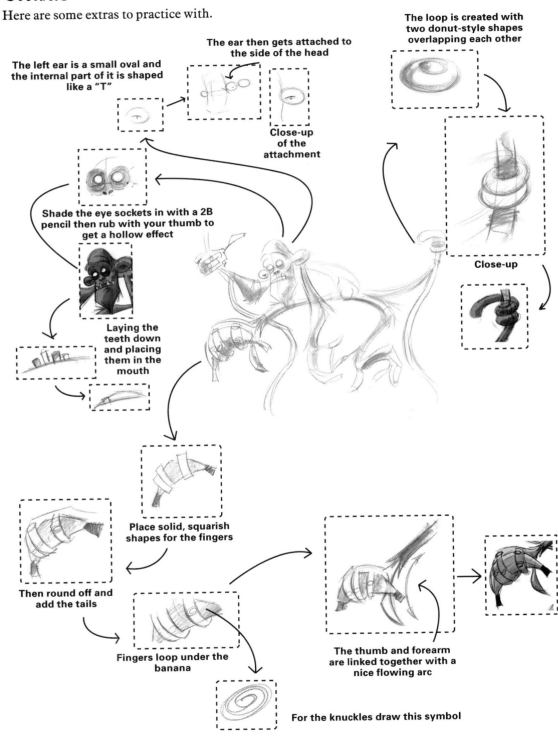

The left ear is a small oval and the internal part of it is shaped like a "T"

The ear then gets attached to the side of the head

Close-up of the attachment

The loop is created with two donut-style shapes overlapping each other

Close-up

Shade the eye sockets in with a 2B pencil then rub with your thumb to get a hollow effect

Laying the teeth down and placing them in the mouth

Place solid, squarish shapes for the fingers

Then round off and add the tails

Fingers loop under the banana

The thumb and forearm are linked together with a nice flowing arc

For the knuckles draw this symbol

Chapter 5
Pirate Extras

Gold 'n' Jewelry
Treasure Chest

Step One
Base

Begin by drawing the base for the chest. This will be the start of a 3D box.

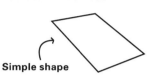

Simple shape

Step Two
The Corners

Erect four corners.

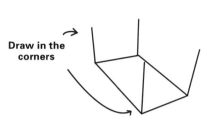

Draw in the corners

Step Three
The Top

All you will be doing here is bringing the base straight up from the bottom.

Copy the base and place it on top

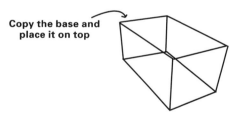

Step Four
The Lid

Add the lid and connect it to the box.

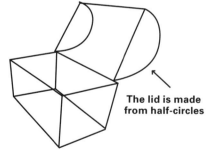

The lid is made from half-circles

Drawing a Pile of Gold

Now that you have created a solid structure, you can add some gold. Begin with a semi-circle as shown, then go ahead and start to populate the mound with gold coins.

Draw the mound with a half-circle

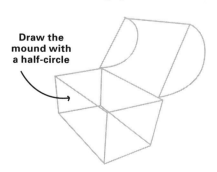

Populate with gold

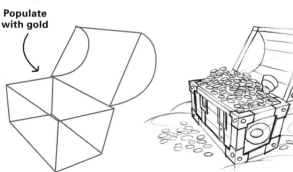

Jewelry

Pirates won't admit it but they wear jewelry, ranging from earrings to gold charms. Here are a few items that you can draw to practice your skills.

Female Pirate Earring

Step One
Draw a dotted line.

Step Two
Draw a circle inside the triangle.

Keep it light

Step Three
Add the beads.

Beads

Celtic Pirate Skull 'n' Bones Necklace

Step One
Start with a guide line.

Skulls will go here

Step Two

Draw two lines on an angle that represent the necklace, then sketch in the ovals that will be used for the skulls.

Step Three
Now add the bones.

Bones

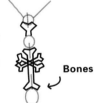

Skull 'n' Bones Earring

Step One
Start with a guide line.

Step Two

At the end of the guide line draw in a two circles; one will be for the skull.

Skull goes here

Step Three

Beads

From here you can start to sketch in the beads with basic shapes.

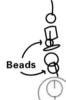

Ancient Medieval Coin

Step One
Construct two guide lines as shown.

Step Two
Sketch in a circle.

Step Three
Add the small metal part that sits on top of the coin.

Pirate Brooch with Skull

Step One
Construct two guide lines as shown.

Step Two
Sketch in the bigger circle first, then the smaller one.

Step Three
Now this next part could be tricky because of the skull that needs to be added, so take your time and draw in the detail.

Skull goes here

Extra detail

Pirate Ring with Skulls

Step One
Draw a basic oval shape for the inner part of the ring.

Step Two
Now draw the outer part of the ring with a small oval for where the skull will sit.

Step Three
Now finish off with jewels.

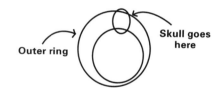

Outer ring

Skull goes here

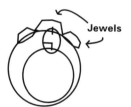

Jewels

Pirate Bone and Coin Necklace

Step One
Draw the guide lines as shown.

Step Two
Now sketch in two circles with a horizontal guide line going through them.

Step Three
Now finish off with the bones.

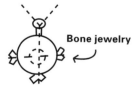

Bone jewelry

Tip: To draw detail well, you need to SLOW down and take your time because the more you look at an object, the better your drawing will become.

Hairdos, Man Beards and Faces

"Ahoy captain! You may want to invest in another barrel of moisturizer for the lads."

Musket Ball Seamus

Hairdo Type: Dreads   **Beard Type:** Goatee

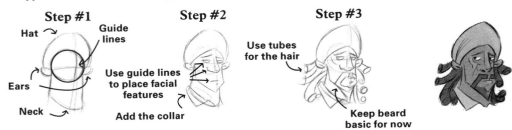

Step #1 — Hat, Guide lines, Ears, Neck

Step #2 — Use guide lines to place facial features, Add the collar

Step #3 — Use tubes for the hair, Keep beard basic for now

1. Sketch in the circle, then a basic tube shape for the neck and add some shoulders.

2. Use the guide lines to place the eyes and mark out where the nose and mouth will sit. The basic shape of the hair can be drawn in now.

3. Those big circular curly bits are not ears—they are part of his man wig. Add some more detail for the nose and mouth.

Cap'n Bernard Mauvebeard

Hairdo Type: Receding Hair   **Beard Type:** Pork Chops + Goatee

Step #1 — Draw circle first, Tube for neck

Step #2 — Start jaw here, Finish jaw here, Collar

Step #3 — "Toof", Basic shape for the beard

1. Start with a light circle, add the guide lines, then draw in a tube for the neck.

2. Draw the shape of the jaw, starting from the right eye and working your way around to the left ear, and then add the eyes, nose and mouth.

3. Now you can start adding the shapes of his massive PORK chops (sideburns, beard). Keep it simple for now.

Captain Hidalgo Dagger

Hairdo Type: Bald Eagle   **Beard Type:** Full-blown Beard

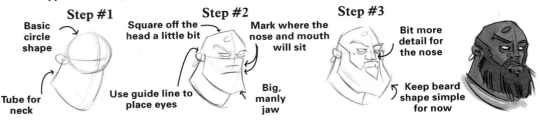

Step #1 — Basic circle shape, Tube for neck

Step #2 — Square off the head a little bit, Use guide line to place eyes, Mark where the nose and mouth will sit, Big, manly jaw

Step #3 — Bit more detail for the nose, Keep beard shape simple for now

1. Start with a light circle, add the guide lines, draw in a tube for the neck and place the right ear on the guide line.

2. On the drawn guide line, place the two eyes and mark where the nose and mouth will sit. Sketch in the jaw.

3. Over the jaw shape, add the beard's basic shape.

Captain George Lowther

Hairdo Type: Balding **Beard Type:** Big Fat Pork Chops

1. Begin with the usual circular shape, with a center guide line and a nose/mouth guide line. Now go over the circle and add a jaw, and from the jaw extend a tube shape to indicate a neck.

2. Place facial features such as the eyes, nose and mouth on the guide line. Mark out a shape for his moustache and mouth.

3. Extend his pork chops out farther with a few simple shapes, and start to define the details now. Press a little harder on the pencil.

Charlotte De Berry

Hairdo Type: Curly and Bushy **Beard Type:** N/A

1. Start with a light circle, and then off that circle construct a jaw and a tube for the neck.

2. Begin the hair with some rough construction shapes to get the proportions correct and then add some basic details for the face.

3. For the curls, draw random circles over the main shape.

Pirate Hand Morgan Sugarfoot

Hairdo Type: Aging but Still There **Beard Type:** Bushy Gray...

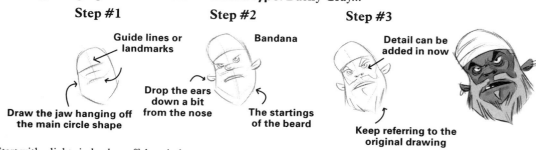

1. Start with a light circle, then off that circle construct a jaw.

2. Place the facial features on the guide lines, keeping the ears below the nose this time. Draw the mouth slightly open. Draw in shape of the bandana.

3. Sketch in a light shape for the beard. Also look closely at the finished version to see if it's the same shape.

Snifflin' Jake Hornigold

Hairdo Type: Swish Back English Man Wig   **Beard Type:** N/A

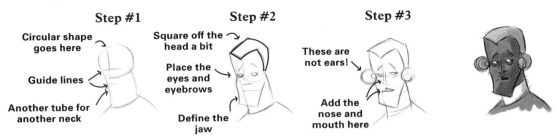

Step #1
Circular shape goes here
Guide lines
Another tube for another neck

Step #2
Square off the head a bit
Place the eyes and eyebrows
Define the jaw

Step #3
These are not ears!
Add the nose and mouth here

1. Sketch in the circle, then a basic tube shape for the neck and add some shoulders.

2. Use the guide lines to place the eyes and mark out where the nose and mouth will sit. The basic shape of the hair can be drawn in now.

3. Those big circular curly parts are not ears—they are part of his man wig. Add some more detail for the nose and mouth.

Oldman Blaine Kidd

Hairdo Type: Bandana   **Beard Type:** Full-Blown Man Beard

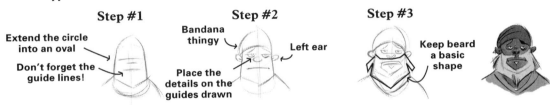

Step #1
Extend the circle into an oval
Don't forget the guide lines!

Step #2
Bandana thingy
Left ear
Place the details on the guides drawn

Step #3
Keep beard a basic shape

1. Start with a circle and then extend the circle to indicate where the neck area is. Roughly draw where the collar is.

2. Draw in the shape of the bandana and then place the facial features on the guide lines. Notice that the ears are in line with the eyes.

3. Start sketching in the beard with a basic beard-like shape. Don't worry too much about the detail yet because you want to make sure the features are in the correct place.

Esmerelda Truelove

Hairdo Type: Girly Long Hair with Curls   **Beard Type:** None that I can see...

Step #1
Circle
Jaw
Extend the neck with a tube

Step #2
Plan your hair with basic shapes
Add facial features
Curls

Step #3
Add some detail to her hair

1. We will begin with the usual circular shape, with a center guide line and a nose/mouth guide line. Now go over the circle and add a jaw. From the jaw extend a tube shape to indicate a neck.

2. Sketch in a light guide line to help you later to draw the hair. Add some shoulders as well.

3. You can now start adding in detail for the hair and other parts of the face.

Mad Nathaniel Basingstoke

Hairdo Type: Blond Dreads   **Beard Type:** Stubble

Step #1

Place eyes on guide lines

Landmarks for the mouth

Circle and tubes

Step #2

One single ear

Big, manly jaw

Step #3

Keep hair shape basic at first

1. Sketch in the circle and then a basic tube shape for the neck. Draw in the guides.

2. Place the eyes on the guide line, along with the nose and mouth. Sketch in the jaw and ear.

3. Block out the hair with some rough hair shapes—just enough to see if it looks good.

Black Bartholomew Scarlett

Hairdo Type: Blonde Short   **Beard Type:** Sideburns and Goatee

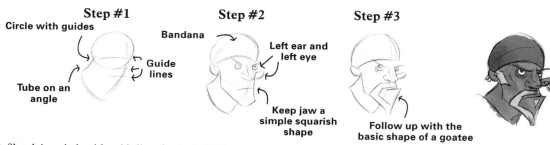

Step #1

Circle with guides

Tube on an angle

Guide lines

Step #2

Bandana

Left ear and left eye

Keep jaw a simple squarish shape

Step #3

Follow up with the basic shape of a goatee

1. Sketch in a circle with guide lines for the facial features, and then draw a tube on an angle that represents the neck.

2. Lightly draw in the jaw with a basic shape and begin to add the eyes and nose. Follow up with both ears. Take note of where the left ear is sitting (a bit below the left eye).

3. Now add the shape of his goatee and sideburns, and keep these basic for now. You can start adding detail when you think you have drawn in all of the basic shapes for the face.

James Kelly Squire

Hairdo Type: Bald as an Eagle   **Beard Type:** Stubble and Goatee

Step #1

Basic shapes first

Lots of rough lines help!

Construction lines for later

Step #2

Use the guide lines to place the facial features

Just a basic shape for the nose

Step #3

Start defining details

Goatee

1. Sketch in a circle with guide lines for the facial features, and then draw a tube that represents the neck.

2. Now start to add the eyes, nose and mouth shapes on the provided guide lines. Sketch out the top part of the chest.

3. Start working on the details for the facial features and start darkening the lines you want to keep. For example, when drawing the eye, you could make it a little darker underneath and then add some wrinkles around it to give the eye an aged look. Or when adding earrings, make sure they are randomly placed around the ear.

Roche Brasiliano

Hairdo Type: Afro/Bushy   **Beard Type:** Trimmed All-Around

Step #1

Rough circle is drawn first

Big tube shape for the neck

Step #2

Keep hair shape simple for now

Both ears are in line with each other

Note the angle of the eyebrows

Step #3

Add more detail at this stage

Start working on more detail for the beards

1. Start with a light circle, then construct the neck with a tube. Add guide lines.

2. Place the facial features on the guide lines, keeping the ears in line with each other. Use the nose as a starting point for the eyebrows, and take note of the angles used. The hair can be a simple shape for now.

3. Start to add more curls for the hair and sketch in a shape for the beard. Once you are happy with it, add more detail and use darker lines.

Thomas Paine

Hairdo Type: Baldy   **Beard Type:** Stubble

Step #1

Create a circle and tube

The ears

Neck

Step #2

Place eyes on guide lines

Start your mouth here

Indicates the Adam's apple

Step #3

Don't forget the earrings

Simple shape for the teeth

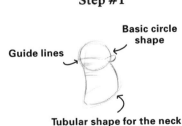

1. Start with a light circle, then construct the neck with a tube. Add guide lines and the basic shape of the ears.

2. Place the eyes, nose and mouth on the guide lines you have just created and define the jaw more clearly.

3. Place a simple shape inside the mouth for the teeth and start to define the details of the face with darker lines.

Captain Kennit

Hairdo Type: Long Hair   **Beard Type:** Nicely Trimmed Beard

Step #1

Guide lines

Basic circle shape

Tubular shape for the neck

Step #2

Draw a circle for the hat

Step #3

Define the hat with darker lines

Use basic shapes to start with

1. Start with a light circle, then construct the neck with a tube. Add guide lines and the basic shape of the ears.

2. For the hat, begin with a circle and don't be afraid of drawing through the head with it. Place the facial features on the guide lines that you have drawn.

3. Sketch in some basic shapes for the beard and hair.

Hats

Below are a few of the many hats that were used by people in the pirate era. Use them as a resource and a starting point to trigger ideas for your characters' style.

The Sideways Flat Pirate Hat

The Wrap-Around Pirate Hat

Deckhand Cap

Beautiful Mistress Hat

Some Sort of Captain Hat

Female Peasant Hat

Female Trader Hat

Male Peasant Hat

Royal Navy Captain Hat

Royal Navy Soldier Hat

Holding Weapons

Eventually, one day very soon, you will be designing characters that will be needing to hold something, whether it is a handful of jelly beans or a hand holding a handful of gold. In this section you are going to see how I visualize and break down the steps and shapes I use to draw characters holding objects.

Holding a Gun

Step One
The Handle and Barrel

Sketch in the main basic shapes of the gun. Use a tube for the barrel and cone/tube for the handle.

Both tubular shapes

Barrel

Handle

Step Two
Drawing the Hands

Now for the tricky part. Start with breaking the fingers into basic rectangles and laying them over the barrel. For the hand holding the handle, draw another basic shape for the trigger finger and a square shape for the fleshy part.

Square shape for the fleshy part

Keep fingers simple for now

Keep it all light sketch strokes

Step Three
Details

This is where you need to look carefully and study the original drawing for the details, so it's a good idea to slow down a little. If you take the time, you can draw some quality stuff.

Add detail carefully

Start to draw darker when happy with line work

Holding a Boarding Axe

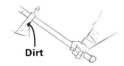

Step One
The Handle

Construct the handle with a long tube.

Long tube

Step Two
Blade and Fingers

Lightly sketch the basic shape of the fingers over the lower part of the handle. Next add the blade at the top of the axe.

Axe blade

Arm

Simple shapes for the fingers

Step Three
Details

Go ahead and start to add the detail, by looking carefully at my drawing.

Dirt

Holding a Standard Sword

Step One
The Handle
Most handles tend to begin with a tube.

Basic tube shape

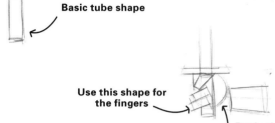

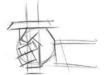

Step Two
Adding the Fingers
Use basic rectangular shapes for the fingers and overlay them across the handle. Draw in a circle for the fleshy part of the hand.

Use this shape for the fingers

Begin the hand with a circle

Step Three
Finishing With the Details
Look carefully at the final drawing and then finish with some details such as the fingernails. I like to give the nails a yellow or greyish tinge that make them really stand out.

Now start to add details

And Another Sword...

Before adding the sword, think about the angle it's going to be held at. Next, sketch in a light guide line representing this angle. Then go ahead and draw over the angle by adding the shape of the sword.

Step One
The Handle
Most handles tend to begin with a tube. With this drawing, try and get the handle on the correct angle.

Place the tube on an angle

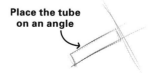

Step Two
Basic Shapes
Block out the major shapes of the arm and hand over the handle.

Draw the big shapes first

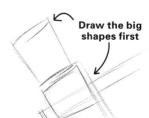

Step Three
Finishing off With the Details
Look carefully at the final drawing and then finish off with some detail, such as the clothing on the arm.

Add the detail now

And Yet Another Sword

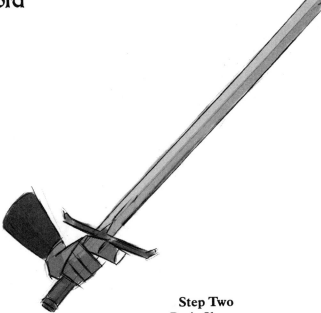

Step One
The Handle
Most handles tend to begin with a tube.

Tube for the handle

Step Two
Basic Shapes
It's a good idea to block out the main shapes. In this drawing, you have a tube for the arm and some squarish shapes fore the three fingers and forefinger. Don't be afraid to draw over the handle, making sure that it has clearance on both sides.

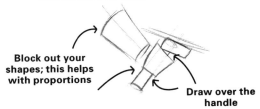

Block out your shapes; this helps with proportions

Draw over the handle

Step Three
Details
The fingers can be drawn in as shown and the forefinger can have its fingernail drawn on for realism.

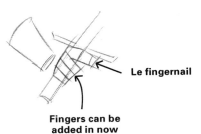

Le fingernail

Fingers can be added in now

Hooks, Eye Patches and Peg Legs

In this tutorial I have decided to give this war-torn pirate amputee an upgrade, with a new eye patch, a peg leg and a shiny new hook. Take a look at the drawing that I have done for you so you can fix up your favorite pirate!

Step One
The Head

Let's begin this character with a circle and a rectangular shape for the chin, then add the guide lines.

Think basic shapes

Step Two
Facial Details and Torso

Now you can start to add some facial details such as the eyes, ears and hair. The bandana can also be added now. For the torso, begin with two circles: one for the chest and the other for the pelvis area. Draw the center line in.

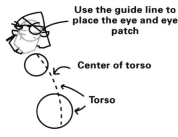

Use the guide line to place the eye and eye patch

Center of torso

Torso

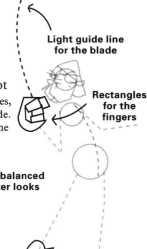

The Eye Patch

Step #1	Step #2	Step #3
Construct the basic shapes.	Add the bandana.	Draw a diagonal line over the bandana and finish by looping it around the head by the ear.

Step Three
The Limbs

Very lightly sketch in the arms and legs with guide lines.

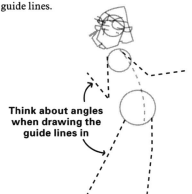

Think about angles when drawing the guide lines in

Step Four
The Right Hand, Sword and Foot

The fingers can be drawn as basic rectangles, then draw the center guide for the blade. The foot can be placed at the bottom of the right leg.

Light guide line for the blade

Rectangles for the fingers

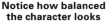

Notice how balanced the character looks

Step Five
Tubes for the Limbs/Hook

Okay, this is where we start getting into the juicy bits. For the arms you will see two different sized tubes. One is the actual arm and the bigger two are the sleeves. So have a go and draw them in first. Now add the hook and finish off the sword. The tubes can be drawn in for the legs. Take note of the peg leg as the tube is a lot smaller.

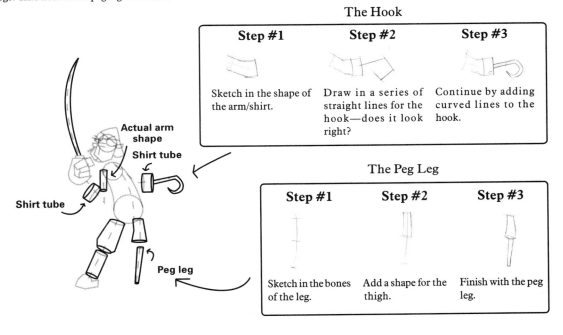

The Hook

Step #1
Sketch in the shape of the arm/shirt.

Step #2
Draw in a series of straight lines for the hook—does it look right?

Step #3
Continue by adding curved lines to the hook.

The Peg Leg

Step #1
Sketch in the bones of the leg.

Step #2
Add a shape for the thigh.

Step #3
Finish with the peg leg.

Actual arm shape

Shirt tube

Shirt tube

Peg leg

Character Breakdown

This is what your drawing should look like at the halfway point. Having lots of rough lines to choose from will help in the long run.

Notice how I "DRAW" through other parts of the body. This is to help keep the proportions consistent.

The Tattooed Pirate

If yer ain't got a tattoo, then yer ain't a proper pirate...so the boys don't care what it is, just go ahead and get one!

Drawing the Tattoo on the Shoulder/Arm

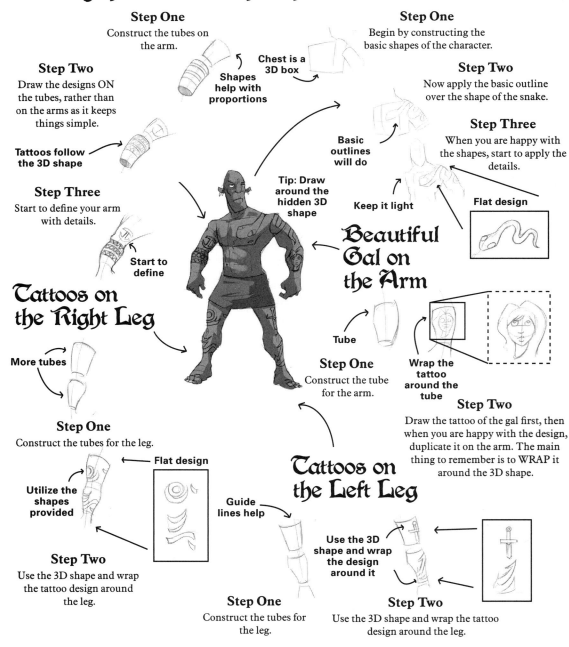

Step One
Construct the tubes on the arm.

Chest is a 3D box

Shapes help with proportions

Step One
Begin by constructing the basic shapes of the character.

Step Two
Draw the designs ON the tubes, rather than on the arms as it keeps things simple.

Tattoos follow the 3D shape

Step Two
Now apply the basic outline over the shape of the snake.

Step Three
When you are happy with the shapes, start to apply the details.

Basic outlines will do

Step Three
Start to define your arm with details.

Start to define

Tip: Draw around the hidden 3D shape

Keep it light

Flat design

Beautiful Gal on the Arm

Tattoos on the Right Leg

More tubes

Tube

Step One
Construct the tube for the arm.

Wrap the tattoo around the tube

Step Two
Draw the tattoo of the gal first, then when you are happy with the design, duplicate it on the arm. The main thing to remember is to WRAP it around the 3D shape.

Step One
Construct the tubes for the leg.

Flat design

Utilize the shapes provided

Tattoos on the Left Leg

Guide lines help

Use the 3D shape and wrap the design around it

Step Two
Use the 3D shape and wrap the tattoo design around the leg.

Step One
Construct the tubes for the leg.

Step Two
Use the 3D shape and wrap the tattoo design around the leg.

How to Draw Designs Wrapped Around a Tube

When wrapping a design around a tube shape such as an arm or a leg, first you need to think of what it would look like in a "straight-on view."

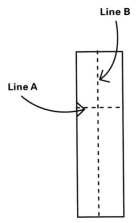

Line B

Line A

Tube Straight-on View

This example started with a simple, straight-on design. In Sample A, when we tilt the tube up, Line A will bend to indicate that the surface and shape are round. In Sample B, the tube is tilted in a downward fashion and Line A follows the shape of the oval, indicating that the tube is round.

Tube Tilted

Sample A   **Sample B**

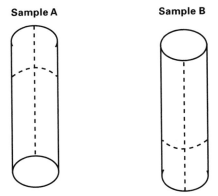

Imagine that the tubes are legs!

The next level is when you have something with a bit more detail. Practice these steps if you are having trouble with the tattoos. The main thing to remember is to "wrap" your designs "around" the arm or leg.

Weapons

Every ship-jumpin' pirate needs some sort of gun to get him through the beastly battles he finds himself in!

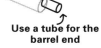

The Flintock Pistol

The flintock pistol is the foundation of all modern guns and has been around for a few hundred years! It's a must-have for any newbie pirate lookin' to yield his/her first booty!

Step One

Begin your flintock pistol with a basic tube shape. Remember to KEEP IT LIGHT!

Basic tube

Step Two

Add another tube for the end of the barrel.

Use a tube for the barrel end

Step Three

For the handle, create a tube that is slightly bent, as this will be the beginnings of it joining with the barrel.

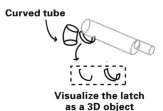

Curved tube

Visualize the latch as a 3D object

Step Four

Use the illustrations provided to get a better understanding on how I went from shapes to detail. When you are happy with your shapes and they look as if they are in the correct place, go ahead and start to darken your line work.

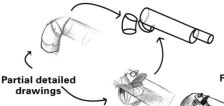

Partial detailed drawings

Final picture

The Musket

Every Royal Navy soldier gets one of these suckers before embarking on a worldwide hunt for those dirty pirates.

Step One

Begin your musket with a directional line as shown below.

Directional line

Step Two

Begin with a basic squarish shape for the barrel.

Light basic shape

Step Three

Add two more shapes: one for the center piece and the other for the handle.

Keep the proportions correct

Step Four

Add the hammer and trigger.

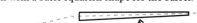

Hammer

Trigger

The Mighty Cannon

Before you go and start a battle with the enemy, it's probably a good idea to think about installing a few cannons in the middle of yer ship!

Step One

The cannon sits on a wooden box to give it height and support for when it shoots, so begin your drawing with a simple 3D box on an angle. Note that the dotted lines represent the edges BEHIND the box.

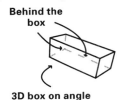

Behind the box

3D box on angle

Step Two
Placing the Wheels

Now is a good time to start visualizing through the box. Place guide lines to represent the axels of the cannon. Doing this can help you place the wheels on the other side if needed. Now draw in the two wooden wheels. Take a look at the breakdown I inserted on how to draw a wheel.

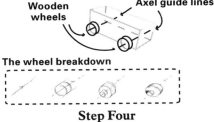

Wooden wheels **Axel guide lines**

The wheel breakdown

Step Three
Attaching the Cannon

The cannon has been created with a basic tube shape that sits on the box we drew earlier. Take a look at the rendered cannon for ideas on how to go from a flat 2D tube to a rounded 3D tube with shading applied to it.

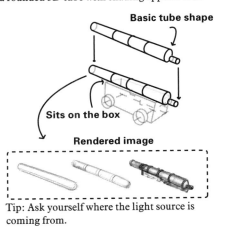

Basic tube shape

Sits on the box

Rendered image

Tip: Ask yourself where the light source is coming from.

Step Four
The Cannon Balls

Here is a great tip on how to draw any sort of balls stacked on each other. Begin with a 3D shape of a pyramid/triangle. This can be your boundary, so try not to go outside of this. Then draw the cannon balls as shown. When you have stacked the cannon balls on each other, use the rendered cannon ball tutorial to add some volume.

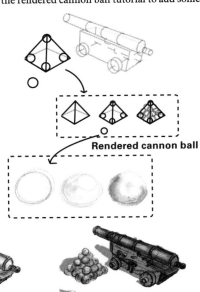

Rendered cannon ball

Final stages

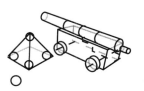

Chapter 6
The Pirate World

The Pirate Fort

Every pirate needs his own fort, even if it's just used to sleep away the rum hangover from the night before.

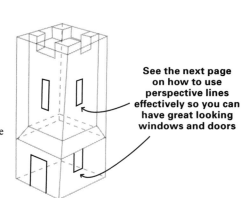

Step One

Begin your pirate fort with a 3D box as drawn here. The dashed lines represent what's behind the box.

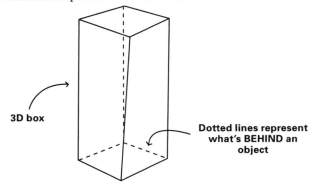

3D box

Dotted lines represent what's BEHIND an object

Step Two

Within the new box you will need to add the guide lines for the lower level of the fort. A technique that I like is to use LINE A and duplicate it for the new guide line, LINE B.

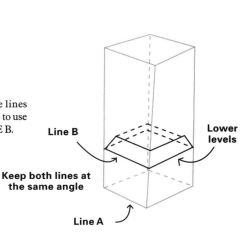

Line B

Lower levels

Keep both lines at the same angle

Line A

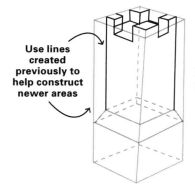

Use lines created previously to help construct newer areas

Step Three

By utilizing the lower guide lines you have just created, you can now begin to draw in the top half of the fort.

Step Four

You can finish off the construction lines with the three windows and the door at the bottom.

See the next page on how to use perspective lines effectively so you can have great looking windows and doors

Using Perspective Lines to Create an Accurate Drawing

Before I attempt to draw an object like this, I think about the angle from which I'm looking at it, and where the perspective points are located. With this drawing, the horizon line is ABOVE the fort. You can tell because we are able to see the TOP of the fort.

Horizon line

This is the horizon line. When you are looking out to sea, the horizon line is where the sky touches the water.

Perspective points are far right and left

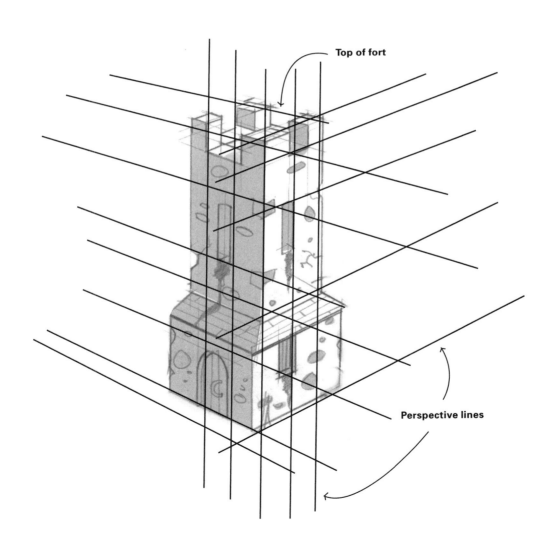

Top of fort

Perspective lines

The Dinghy

Step One

The best way to approach the dinghy is to think of a shoebox. Being able to draw 3D shapes is vital to any artist, so if you can't get it right at the moment, I would recommend practicing the shape first, then coming back to more complicated stuff once you feel comfortable with it.

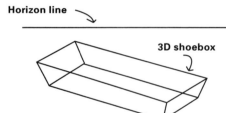

Horizon line

3D shoebox

Step Two

Now that we have a base to work with, you can start to mold the shoebox into a dinghy. You will need to utilize the 3D shape in order to get a great-looking boat. Drawing the center guide line as shown will help you to place the front part accurately.

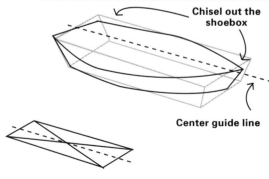

Chisel out the shoebox

Center guide line

Tip: To find the center, draw two diagonal lines in the rectangle so that they cross each other. Where the two lines meet is the center.

An idea of how rough I get when constructing the dinghy

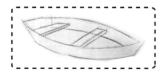

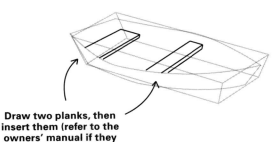

Draw two planks, then insert them (refer to the owners' manual if they don't fit)

Step Three

Every dinghy needs some seats. The ones on this dinghy have been created with 3D rectangles, so just slot them as shown.

Step Four

I used a ruler for both oars, since drawing objects with long straight lines and not using a ruler can sometimes leave them looking pretty rubbery.

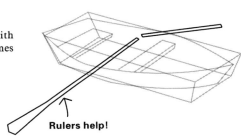

Rulers help!

Adding **Two** Mates to a Dinghy

Create the boat shapes first and don't add the mates in until you have added the seats. This will make it easier to place the characters.

Rough breakdown of two pirate mates

Drawing the mates will be tricky — go back to "Drawing the Pirate" for tips

The Dungeon

Not every pirate can get off scot-free for pillaging other people's boats, and if they do get caught, where do you think they end up? You guessed it...the pirate dungeon, which is usually located in the depths of an ancient castle. In this tutorial, you will learn how to create and visualize a dungeon scene, starting from a simple 3D shoebox.

Shoebox

Keep it light

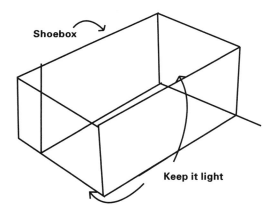

Step One

In a drawing such as this, you have to visualize a major shape such as a shoebox. This gives you a solid boundary to work within. From here you will be able to place objects into the area you have just created. Keep this shape as light as possible, because we will not use all of the lines.

Step Two

Creating a doorway is tricky enough, let alone a doorway on an angle! See the little demo below for how I accomplished this.

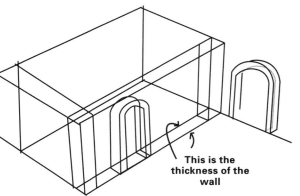

This is the thickness of the wall

Drawing the Doorway

Step #1
Create a 3D box as drawn.

Step #2
Draw in the front part of the doorway. Use the box that you have drawn.

Step #3
Duplicate the same doorway for the rear part.

Step #4
Darken your lines.

Step #5
Add your detail, then clean up your door.

Step Three

You can now begin to add details to the drawing. It doesn't matter where you start, just jump in! The key here is to slow down and really LOOK at what you are drawing. DON'T draw what you think you see. Take the time to study what you are copying.

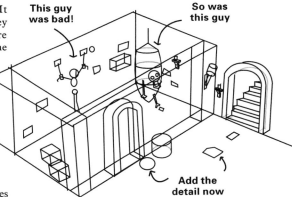

This guy was bad!

So was this guy

Add the detail now

Step Four

This next step is learning how to transition from shapes and lines to adding detail. Here is a drawing I did after finishing off the guide lines I drew earlier. It's very important to know that this stage is more of an "ideas stage" rather than a "this drawing must look nice stage." This is where you experiment with your ideas and techniques.

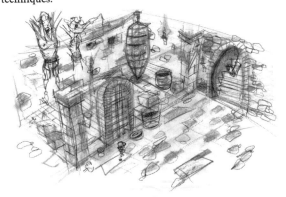

Rough drawing

Step Five

This is the cleaned-up version that is ready to be colored. The technique I use is laying a new piece of paper over the rough drawing and redrawing it with a sharp pencil.

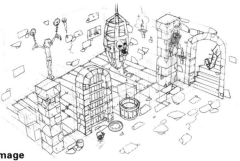

Redrawn image

Drawing a Palm Tree

Every pirate needs an island, and every island needs some palm trees, so let's go ahead and draw some.

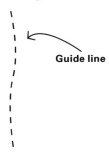

Guide line

Step One
Begin with a vertical guide line indicating the center of the palm tree.

Tubes will help

Step Two
Add tubes for the trunk.

Use dotted lines to help place the leaves

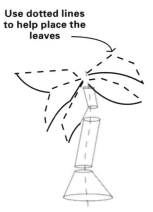

Step Three
Start with a guide line (see dotted line) for the center of the leaf, then draw the underbelly of it.

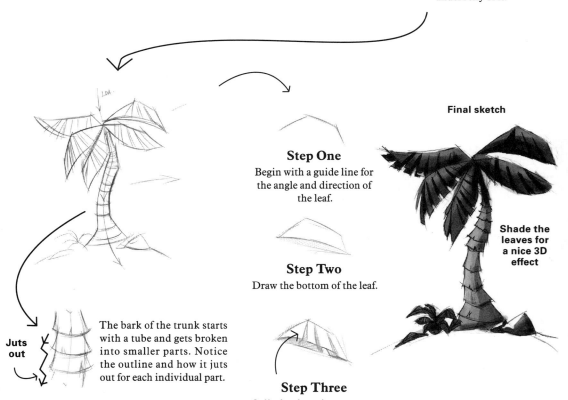

Juts out

The bark of the trunk starts with a tube and gets broken into smaller parts. Notice the outline and how it juts out for each individual part.

Step One
Begin with a guide line for the angle and direction of the leaf.

Step Two
Draw the bottom of the leaf.

Step Three
Split the shape into parts to look like individual leaves.

Final sketch

Shade the leaves for a nice 3D effect

Drawing a Pirate Shack

In order to pillage an island, a pirate must set up base—hence the Pirate Shack. This type of shack is commonly used for sleepin' 'n' drinkin' and the occasional eatin'. Then, after all that, they can get on and do some pillagin'... arrrrrr.

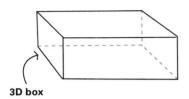

3D box

Step One

First, begin your shack with a 3D box. The dashed lines represent what's BEHIND the shack.

Roof goes here

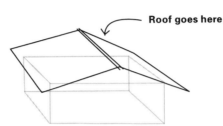

Step Two

Place the roof in its correct location on top of the shack.

These are the poles

Step Three

Draw in the door and the side window, followed by the overhang with the two poles holding it up.

The window has been created with a series of lines as shown here. Draw these in first with a ruler and be sure to keep it light. When you are happy with the angles, finish off the window.

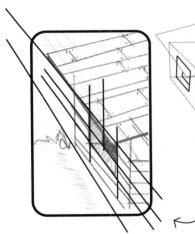

To make objects appear visually interesting to the human eye, try and add as much detail as you can. I have done this for the roof. You might say, "Dude, it's only a roof." Then I will say "Well, no, it's actually a roof with rivets and uneven planks that look as if they have been installed by an intoxicated pirate." Which one do you think is more interesting? Remember to try and tell a story for everything that you draw!

The Pirate Island

When designing your own island to pillage, there are a few things you need to think of before going gung-ho with detail. The first MAIN obstacle is the angle. Is it going to be at eye level, or a map-like straight down or like the three-quarter view that I have drawn? So, sharpen your pencils and yer brain and let's get drawing before the sun sets and we got no place to drink rum.

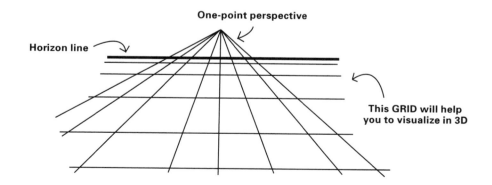

One-point perspective

Horizon line

This GRID will help you to visualize in 3D

Step One

In this type of drawing we will use PERSPECTIVE on a PLANE. A plane can be described as the surface of an object or land. In this scenario, we will be using water and land as our PLANE. What you see here are three elements that begin the drawing: the horizon line, one-point perspective and a grid. The thick line is the HORIZON line, which is also the EYE line. The lines starting at the top and spreading out as they get closer to us are the PERSPECTIVE lines. Finally, the thin horizontal lines coming down the page help us to visualize and create DISTANCE.

Step Two

The next step is to add the island over the grid we have just created. I have utilized the perspective lines to create the impression of distance and depth, which means making objects smaller as they get farther away. Go ahead and copy what I have drawn and remember to keep it light!

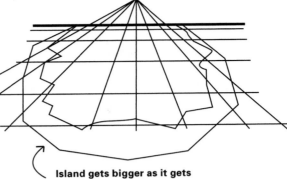

Island gets bigger as it gets closer to you

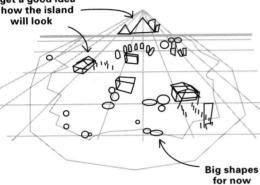

Use basic shapes to get a good idea of how the island will look

Big shapes for now

Step Three

In this step you can start to add small amounts of detail. I have started with the shacks, mountains and rocks. I have sketched them in as basic shapes for now, because I want to see if the composition works. Later, I will refine what I have drawn.

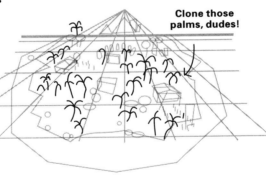

Clone those palms, dudes!

Step Four

This is where your patience will be tested as drawing one thing over and over can be quite tedious! Randomly place palm trees over the island as shown. The following pages will demonstrate how to draw a palm tree at a larger scale.

Pencil sketch before you color in

Ye Olde Pirate Map

As a pillaging pirate, where would ye hide all yer gold?
At the local bank? I think not! A pirate map comes in
handy at the worst of times, when you have run out of
pennies and you need to remember where you buried the
loot. As you can see, there is not too much writing on the
map since most pirates can't read anyway. So, what are ye
waiting for? Starting searching!

Step One

We shall begin with drawing a border so you have
boundaries to work within. You can make this shape
slightly off, if it pleases you.

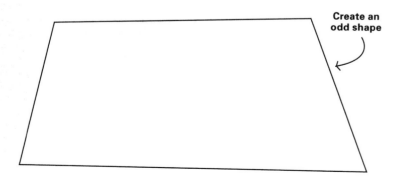

**Create an
odd shape**

Step Two

When you pick up yer map from the local mapmaker down in the village, it's going to be rolled up. When you unroll it, it's going to look like this. If you are lucky, you may even get the version with ripped edges, such as mine!

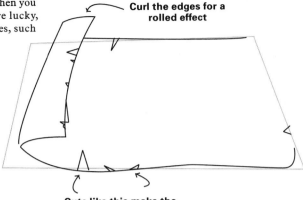

Curl the edges for a rolled effect

Cuts like this make the map look old

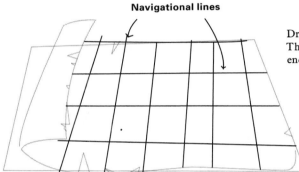

Navigational lines

Step Three

Draw in some horizontal and vertical lines on your map. These represent longitude and latitude, which, in the end, will help the pirate figure out where he/she is!

Step Four

Sketch in the navigational image in the top right-hand corner. You can now start to add the details on the map. Maps tend to be old and weathered, so it's a good idea to add rips and water stains around the edges. Most maps also have a compass to indicate which way is north, and latitude and longitude lines to help sea-faring pirates locate their treasures! Another important detail is to throw in a couple of palm trees when you're drawing islands to indicate shrubbery and foliage.

Detail can now be added

Ye Olde Pirate Port

Lookin' to get rid of the loot you pillaged earlier? Well, look no farther, as you have just arrived at a Pirate Port for Pillaging. This is a great tutorial for learning how to place a house on a piece of land and how to visualize this land as a 3D plane.

Step One

For a drawing such as this, a 3D plane can help you plan the rest of the drawing. A plane is a grid on an angle.

Create a grid

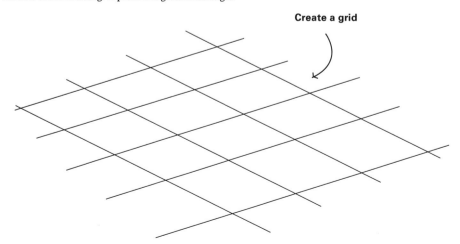

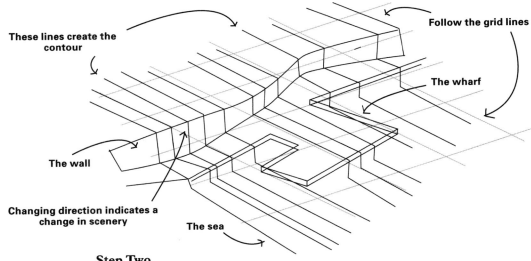

These lines create the contour

Follow the grid lines

The wharf

The wall

Changing direction indicates a change in scenery

The sea

Step Two

This next step is figuring out the CONTOUR of the area. The contour is the outline, or, in this case, the surface of a drawing. This helps the artist visualize a drawing better. Follow the initial grid lines we drew earlier with your new contour lines. When you see the line change angle and direction, this is where there is a change in scenery, such as the wall hitting the wharf and then the wharf hitting the sea.

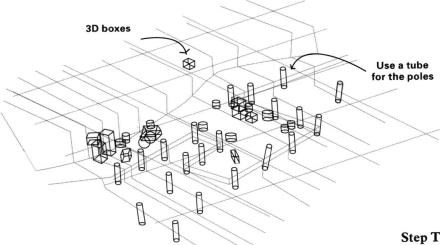

3D boxes

Use a tube for the poles

Step Three

After completing the base of the drawing, you are now ready to add smaller elements to the sketch. Start with the poles in the water. These can be constructed with tubes. The boxes have also been created as 3D objects, so scatter them around randomly.

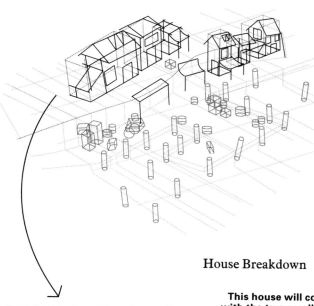

Step Four

This is where you can start to add the housing. Use the guide lines of the plane we drew earlier as starting points. The houses have been created with basic 3D blocks, which can help you to visualize and rotate them later on if you need to.

As we break this drawing down into the various elements, you will notice that I step away from the original drawing and draw the houses by themselves. I can do this because of the 3D aspect. Everything that I draw is 3D. This enables me to see the drawing as a 3D puzzle, clipping things here and moving things there. So try and think in 3D as much as possible.

House Breakdown

Basic 3D block

These lines will help

This house will connect with the two smaller units

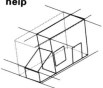

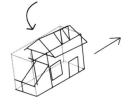

Think 3D puzzle and clip your elements into place

Step #1

Begin with a basic 3D block so we have some boundaries to work within.

Step #2

Using the angles of the 3D block, create the house.

Step #3

Finish of the construction by adding on the roof shape.

I like a lot of rough lines

My clean-up

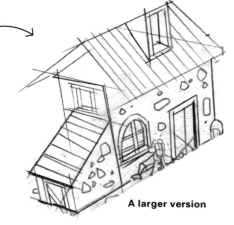

Step #4

Now you can start to get messy and rough out the details of the house. Keep it light, and then when you are happy with the art, go dark.

Step #5

This is the cleaned-up version done on a new piece of paper.

A larger version

Step Five

In this last step, you can add the boats. Think about the little stuff, like tying the boats to the poles and drawing objects that could be in the boats. The more little stuff you add, the better the story you can tell.

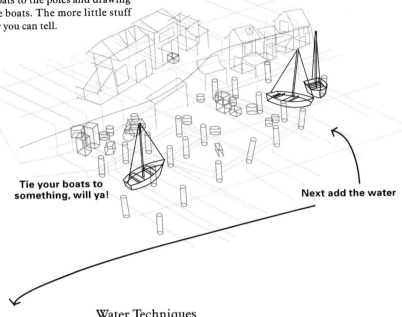

Tie your boats to something, will ya!

Next add the water

Water Techniques

My initial sketch of water interacting with the dock poles

The refined version

The main thing to remember about water is that you won't see it still unless it's a very calm day with no wind. Most of the time, water is being moved by the tide, and when it is close to a port like this one, it will have to hit objects as it moves. In this example, the water is being pushed into the boats and docking poles. Another thing to think about (yes, that's right, more thinking) is the randomness of how the water moves. You can achieve this look by not allowing two or more lines of water to be parallel to each other... confused? See the example below.

Boring and unrealistic

Perfect randomness!

The Pirate Ship

Step One

The best way to start this ship, or any ship, is with a 3D block of cheese, as drawn. Take note of how the back part of the boat is on a slight angle. This is partly because of the perspective I have used. I have also drawn the BACK of the boat with dotted lines.

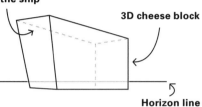

Visualize "behind" the ship

3D cheese block

Horizon line

Step Two

Now that we have a foundation to draw with, you can start to chisel the block of cheese into a semi-decent pirate ship. You can see the 3D segment that I have chiseled out for your enjoyment. Lastly, place the rudder at the back of the boat with it touching the water.

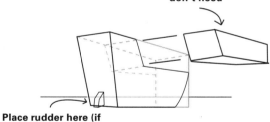

Chisel out what you don't need

Place rudder here (if faulty, please refer to the owner's manual)

Step Three

What does every pirate ship need? That's right, you guessed it. Masts. These hold the sails that make the boat move. Place three masts in their correct places (you may want to use a ruler to get nice, crisp lines). Now add the windows located at the end of the boat and the cannon openings just below them. I have drawn a rectangle at the back of the ship to help me place the rear window later. Lastly, add the two giant lamps.

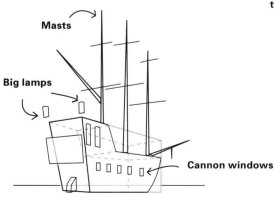

Masts

Big lamps

Cannon windows

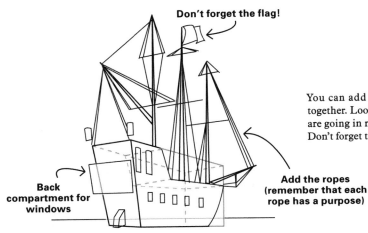

Don't forget the flag!

Back compartment for windows

Add the ropes (remember that each rope has a purpose)

Step Four

You can add the ropes that hold the masts and sails together. Look carefully, because it may appear as if they are going in random places, but each rope has a purpose. Don't forget to add the flag at the top of the ship.

Step Five

This next step is to illustrate, from guide lines and shapes to adding the details. Hopefully, you have kept the guide lines light so when you do go and add the details the guide lines will just disappear!

Line Art

Drawing Cannons

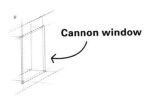

Cannon window

Door

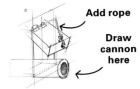

Add rope

Draw cannon here

Step One

Begin by thinking of the environment that the cannon is in. You will need to create a window for the cannon to shoot from.

Step Two

Next, you need to draw the door that protects the cannon when it's not in use. This is a simple 3D box.

Step Three

Lastly, sketch in a tube for the cannon. Make sure that you visualize the inside of the cannon well. Draw the rope and hinges.

Old Pirate Town

Pirates like to have their own space and occasionally choose locations deep in the jungle, where they can hide some of their jewels and gold. In this tutorial, I will break down the process of drawing shacks in a jungle.

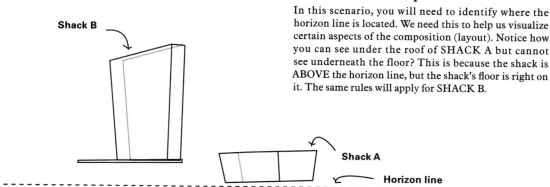

Step One

In this scenario, you will need to identify where the horizon line is located. We need this to help us visualize certain aspects of the composition (layout). Notice how you can see under the roof of SHACK A but cannot see underneath the floor? This is because the shack is ABOVE the horizon line, but the shack's floor is right on it. The same rules will apply for SHACK B.

Step Two

Every shack needs a roof of some sort, so what I have done here is utilize the 3D shape and add a roof within the box. The box helps me to keep the dimensions of the shack correct. With Shack A, there are no guide lines, as I have visualized the box in my head. You can now place the door and windows as shown.

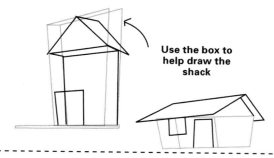

Use the box to help draw the shack

Step Three

If you are a clever pirate, when constructing a shack in water, you will use poles to avoid getting wet. If you are not a clever pirate, you will not use poles to avoid getting wet, you will do the complete opposite. The poles will need to be vertical and drawn so that they are holding up both the main structure as well as anything hanging over. You can now place the ladders. Make sure that they are touching the water and creating a rippling effect.

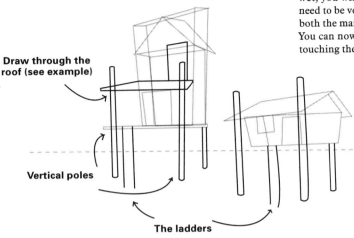

Draw through the roof (see example)

Vertical poles

The ladders

Step Four

Okay, at this stage of the drawing it can get pretty messy, so the best way to combat this is to keep the construction lines as light as possible—we will not use all of them. Drawing trees is a skill set in itself, and I could devote a whole book to it, so do your best here to add trees that are growing underneath and behind the shacks.

Close-up of the shack

Take note of the nails I have added

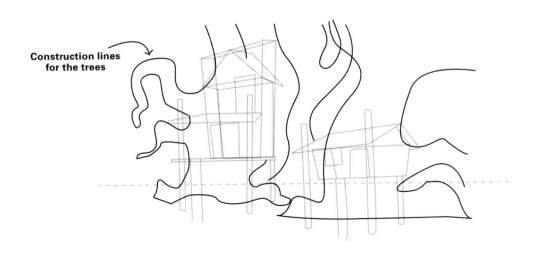

Construction lines for the trees

Step Five

The last stage to this epic drawing is adding final details, such as the leaves, the wooden planks, the vines that loop through the woods and any shading that will enhance the look of the drawing.

Wooden planks

Big looping vines

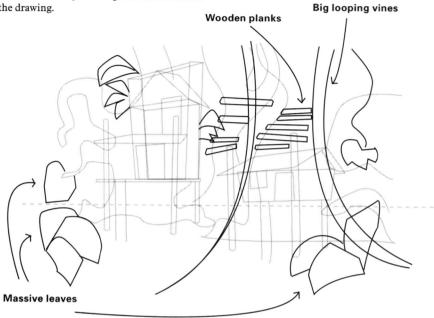

Massive leaves

This is the line art that I scanned into the computer just before I colored it in with Photoshop

Drawing the Shack

Here is some insight on my drawing process when creating a picture like the Pirate Town. You can see at Step #1 that it has a very loose feel, while I am trying to figure out what works and what doesn't. A technique that I use is overlaying a NEW piece of paper on top of the rough drawing and refining the sketch. This technique is repeated until I am happy with the final rendering. I will then proceed to cleaning up the picture and getting it ready to be scanned into the computer to be colored.

A Few Tips to Get You Started on Your Own Pirate Town:

When designing a shack, I scout around the Internet looking for old run-down cabins and then I print them out and pin them to the wall for inspiration and ideas. I use this process for the trees and water to achieve great results. If you don't use reference material for inspiration and ideas, you will find that your drawings look flat and dull.

Step #1
Initial sketch

Step #2
Refined and redrawn

Step #3
Final revision, then scanned

DATE DUE

FEB 1 2 2010			

Demco, Inc. 38-293

Watkins College

00015323